WORMS EAT MY GARBAGE

Flowerfield Enterprises, LLC

Checklist

Reference
page

☐ 1. Read *Worms Eat My Garbage*

☐ 2. Weigh kitchen waste for two to three weeks to
get average amount produced in your household 14-15

☐ 3. Determine quantity of worms you need and
order worms 51-55

☐ 4. Purchase bin or select size of container required
and assemble materials 12-29

☐ 5. Determine what beddings are available, and
either order or scrounge 30-37

☐ 6. Build or assemble bin 16-25

☐ 7. Prepare beddings. If manure, do so at least
two days prior to arrival of worms 56-59

☐ 8. Add worms to bedding 60-61

☐ 9. Bury garbage 60-72

☐ 10. Check moisture periodically; look for
cocoons and young worms 73-75

☐ 11. Harvest worms and prepare new bedding 75-86

☐ 12. Use vermicompost or worm castings on house
plants or in your garden. 110-119

WORMS
Eat My
Garbage

Second Edition

by
Mary Appelhof
with illustrations by
Mary Frances Fenton

Flowerfield Enterprises, LLC
Kalamazoo, Michigan USA

"1-2-3 Worm Box," artist, Mary Frances Fenton, adapted from "Composting your garbage with worms," 1979, with permission of Kalamazoo Nature Center, Kalamazoo, MI.

"Variety of garbage eaten by worms," artist, Mary Frances Fenton, adapted from "Kinds of garbage eaten by worms" in *Winter Composting with Worms*, final report from the Kalamazoo Nature Center to the National Center for Appropriate Technology, 1979.

"Food web of the compost pile," artist, Dan Dindal, from *Ecology of Compost*, State University of New York, College of Environmental Science and Forestry, Syracuse, NY, 1972. Reprinted with permission of the artist.

Publisher's Cataloging-in-Publication
(*Provided by Quality Books, Inc.*)

Appelhof, Mary.
    Worms eat my garbage / by Mary Appelhof ; with illustrations by Mary Frances Fenton ; edited by Diane D. Worden. — 2nd ed., rev. and expanded. — Kalamazoo, Mich. : Flower Press, 1997.
    p. cm.
    Includes bibliographical references and index.
    ISBN: 978-0-9778045-1-1

    1. Earthworm culture. 2. Earthworms. 3. Compost. 4. Compost animals. I. Title

SF597.E3A67 1997   639'.7546
                                      QBI97-888

Flowerfield Enterprises, LLC
10332 Shaver Road
Kalamazoo, Michigan 49024
ISBN 978-0-9778045-1-1

Contents

Checklist..ii

List of figures..vi

Acknowledgments...viii

Foreword ix

Chapters

  1. What should I call it?..................................... 1

  2. Where should I put a worm bin?................... 3

  3. What container should I use?...................... 12

  4. What are worm beddings? 30

  5. What kind of worms should I use? 38

  6. What is the sex life of a worm? 45

  7. How many worms do I need?...................... 51

  8. How do I set up my worm bin? 56

  9. What kind of garbage, and what do I do with it? 62

10. How do I take care of my worms? 73

11. What are the most commonly asked questions
    about worms? 90

12. What are some other critters in my worm bin? 95

13. How do plants benefit from a worm bin? 110

14. How can I treat waste as a resource? 120

Afterword: How many worms in an acre? 128

Appendix A: Record sheet..130

Appendix B: Annotated references 131

Appendix C: A metric scenario 139

Glossary... 142

Bibliography.. 149

Index... 154

About the author...163

List of figures

Figure 1.   Gail Enemark's coffee-table worm bin is
            in her living room.   10

Figure 2.   Shallow containers have more surface
            area for burying waste.   14

Figure 3.   Few materials are needed for a 1-2-3
            Worm Box.   17

Figure 4.   Construction diagram for Worm Box
            includes side overlap on corners.   18

Figure 5.   These materials are needed for a Two-
            Person Bin.   18

Figure 6.   Patio Bench Bin sits on block supports.   19

Figure 7.   More materials are needed for a Patio
            Bench Bin.   20

Figure 8.   Cutting pattern for plywood.   21

Figure 9.   Dimensions of each worm bin part
            in the Patio Bench Bin.   21

Figure 10. Cutting diagram for framing lumber.   22

Figure 11. Board lengths of each worm bin part
            vary in the Patio Bench.   22

Figure 12. Base frame has all 2x4's on edge.   23

Figure 13. Patio Bench Worm Bin is shown
            with lid up.   25

Figure 14. Two of the four tiers of the circular
            Can-O-Worms bin are shown above.   27

Figure 15. Worm-a-way bins feature transverse
            ventilation pipes near the base.   28

Figure 16. Composters live and work in upper
            organic layers of soil.   40

Figure 17. Worms are hermaphroditic.   47

Figure 18. English units for bins and bedding
            are feet, gallons, and pounds.   57

Figure 19. Metric units for bins and bedding are
            centimeters, liters, and kilograms.   57

Figure 20. Actual food waste that was buried
            during a demonstration project.   63

Figure 21. Burial spots are recorded.   69

Figure 22. Dump and hand sort is an effective way
            to separate worms from their castings.   80

Figure 23. Letting the worms sort themselves from
            their castings saves worm workers' time.   84

Figure 24. Divide and dump is a straightforward
            technique.   86

Figure 25. Sam Hambly points out features of his
            bottomless insulated worm bin suitable
            for Canadian winters.   87

Figure 26. Corner detail shows fitted Styrofoam,
            hook, and eyes.   87

Figure 27. Organisms commonly found in compost
            include both plants and animals.   97

Figure 28. Home-made traps are effective.   104

Figure 29. Seeds and young plants benefit from
            nutrients present in vermicompost.   111

Figure 30. Nutrients become available to plants
            when water drips from its leaves.   112

Figure 31. Different potting media affect the health
            of African violets.   114

Acknowledgments

I thank everyone who has helped make this book possible. Since the first edition was published, thousands of people have contributed to advancing my knowledge of worms and their role in transforming materials from one form to another. You have raised questions, given me insights, shared problems, offered solutions. You helped me identify areas where you want to know more.

One gratifying aspect of this open-communication process is that I now have more people to talk with about worms! Another is that there are so many other ways to obtain quality information about worms, including the WorldWideWeb, conferences, workshops (wormshops!), newsletters, articles, and books for adults and children.

I value the contributions of John Buckerfield, soil scientist from CSIRO in Adelaide, Australia, for review of the manuscript and his many helpful suggestions. I am grateful to Diane Worden for her thoroughness and patience in editing and indexing this book. We have collaborated on earthworm projects before, and it is a joy to work again alongside her.

Special thanks go to my operations manager, Nancy Essex, for taking on the task of typesetting. She was willing to tackle the complexities which present themselves when information is transformed from words and pictures, photographs and electronic files, to files the printer can understand. I appreciate her steady and consistent presence.

Nancy and I could not have accomplished what we did without the cheerful work done by the rest of my staff, K'Anna Burton and Linda Redding, handling customer orders, and providing phone support. I appreciate their competence, good nature, flexibility, and dependability.

I thank Dr. Daniel Dindal, for continued use of his "Food Web of the Compost Pile," and Maria Perez-Stable for her proofreading. Finally, I thank Mary Frances Fenton for the illustrations that make this book so unique.

Foreword

Worms eat my garbage. They've been eating it for the past twenty-five years. Before then I used to object to the smell that developed when I dumped coffee grounds, banana peels, table scraps, and other food waste into my kitchen wastebasket. I got rid of the smell in my kitchen when I learned how to compost food waste outdoors by mixing it with grass clippings, leaves, manure, and soil. However, although composting worked fine in the spring, summer, and fall, it was not convenient during a northern winter. Either the ground froze or I'd have to wade through the snow to get to the compost pile. Sometimes, even the compost pile froze! Now I let earthworms help with the composting inside the house, and there is less odor when waste goes into the worms instead of the wastebasket.

Using earthworms and microorganisms to convert organic waste into black, earthy-smelling, nutrient-rich humus is known as **vermicomposting**. I began vermicomposting when I ordered a small quantity of redworms through the mail and started to experiment with them. I placed them in a container in my basement, provided a bedding for the worms, and buried most of my kitchen waste in this bin. Using about a pound of worms, I buried 65 pounds (30kg) of garbage during a 110-day period. When spring came, I used the resulting vermicompost in my garden and discovered that the production of broccoli and tomatoes was much better than I had dreamed possible.

The whole vermicomposting process is very simple and has obvious advantages besides increasing garden yields. Worms don't make noise, and they require very little care. Because I separate the newspapers and packaging, cans, and glass, they never get mixed in with the smelly stuff, and they are cleaner and easier to recycle. I have wonderful fertilizer for my plants; save the money that used to pay for weekly trash pickup; and, oh yes, always have plenty of worms for fishing.

I knew from my own experience by the early 1980's that thousands of people, both children and adults, had seen worms at work in demonstration vermicomposting units at energy fairs, harvest festivals, barter fairs, and garden clubs. Now that number has grown into millions because thousands of worm workers everywhere are showing friends their own worm bins, or taking a portable worm bin to school, or setting up a booth at the county fair to demonstrate how easy it is to process garbage with worms. After an initial, "Yuck!" questions pour out.

Learning about vermicomposting occurs every time I set up a new unit. That practical experience, plus a biology-teaching and research background, helps me evaluate the published information available. It also convinced me to write a detailed, yet simple, manual about vermicomposting. In addition to learning from the worms themselves and the scientists who conduct research about them, I learn more from a myriad of worm workers, a term I coined in 1993 at the first Worm Summit in San Francisco. To the 43 northern Californians assembled in Cindy Nelson's home I said, "I'm calling us 'worm workers.' Worm workers like ourselves use worms to eat our garbage, adapt techniques to meet a wider range of conditions, teach other people how to do it, or raise worms to get them set up." The number of worm workers continues to grow.

The first edition of *Worms Eat My Garbage* in 1982 met the needs of people in 50 states and over 60 foreign countries. After publication it went through 15 printings in as many years, totaling 100,000 copies! I have seen dog-eared and compost-stained library copies that obviously were used as beside-the-bin manuals to get a worm composting system started.

That first edition received many favorable reviews about its readability, its sensible approach, and its societal goals. Reviewers saw it as a practical guide in acting locally and thinking globally. The futurist Hazel Henderson wrote that *Worms Eat My Garbage* was creating a path to the Solar Age. Academics also appreciated it. While at Virginia Polytechnic Institute and State University, Dr. E. Scott Geller predicted that "applying (its) innovative and convenient conservation strategies will be rewarding to you and your environment." He wrote from his own experience; worms ate his garbage, too. Dr. Bethe Hagens of Governor's State University chose to focus on its central thesis, "Waste is a resource out of place—whether it's your kitchen scraps or the manure your worms will produce."

Representing Michigan's 60th District in the state legislature for four consecutive terms, Mary Brown once summarized the impact vermicomposting can have. "Recycling is good ecology, good economics," she wrote. "This guide shows personal commitment to a better use of the waste we generate. A commitment to fewer landfills, more appropriate use of energy, and the return to a more independent, yet socially responsible system of waste disposal." All to be done with tiny worms!

This revision, as the original edition did, still attempts to answer the most common questions. However, it expands on appropriate kinds of worm bin containers, including several available commercially, and gives more information about worms and their associated organisms, based on what increased scientific and commercial interest in vermiculture has brought to the 1990's. The bibliography consequently reflects some of the most recent literature. This edition incorporates metric units to make it easier for those who are unfamiliar with the English units used in the United States. Finally, it contains a more detailed index than the original and all of its reprintings.

I hope this book convinces each reader that you, too, can vermicompost, and that this simple process with the funny name is a lot easier to do than you thought. After all, if worms eat *my* garbage, they will eat yours, too.

1
What should I call it?

Some people use the term "home vermicomposting system" because it sounds more sophisticated than "worm bin." They are right on both counts; it is sophisticated, and it is a system. The system consists of five interdependent parts:

1. **Physical Structure,** a box or container
2. **Biological Organisms,** the worms and their associates
3. **Controlled Environment,** of temperature, moisture, acidity, ventilation
4. **Maintenance Procedures,** for preparing beddings, burying garbage, separating worms from their castings
5. **Production Procedures,** for making use of the castings (worm manure)

I hesitate to use "home vermicomposting system" exclusively because the term itself might frighten away those who feel more comfortable with "worm bin." It sounds less intimidating to suggest taking a plastic container or wooden box and putting holes in it to provide a source of air. Then add damp bedding and worms, bury garbage, harvest worms, and set up fresh bedding as necessary. If calling this system a worm bin encourages you to try the technique, no other term is better.

On the other hand, the system really is complex. Much more can be learned about it: Just what is going on in that bin? Are the worms really eating the garbage? Or are they eating the bacteria, protozoa, molds, and fungi that are breaking down the food waste? Can conditions become too acid? How can you tell? What kinds of food might cause overacidity? When is the best time to harvest if you want the greatest number of worms for the least amount of time and effort? When do you harvest to get the best castings? What is the best-sized container to bury a given quantity of garbage?

If you like to compare notes, for example, about ideal temperature for cocoon production or about acceptable levels of **anaerobiosis**, you might want to say you have a home vermicomposting system. I have such a system. I know a lot about vermicomposting, but I also have a lot more to learn. For myself, I just say, "Worms eat my garbage. Wanna see my worm bin?"

2.
Where should I put a worm bin?

In deciding where to put your worm bin, consider both the worms' needs and your own. That may sound elementary, but I've learned from experience that there are a few basics you should think about in advance. Adjusting your thinking early will help determine later how successful and enjoyable a worm bin is for you.

To make the worms happy, you'll need to think about temperature, moisture, acidity, and ventilation. Equally as important, to make yourself happy, you'll want to consider your expectations, convenience, and aesthetic preferences.

YOUR WORM'S NEEDS

Temperature
You will be using redworms for reasons that I will discuss later. They feed most rapidly and probably convert waste best at temperatures between 59-77°F (15-25°C). They can work their way through garbage in a basement bin with temperatures as low as 50°F (10°C). Redworms tolerate a wide range of temperatures, but below freezing temperatures may kill them. Earthworms have successfully weath-

ered cold northern winters in pits dug into the ground that
were covered with manure, straw, and leaves to provide
heat, food, and insulation. The problem with an outdoor
pit for winter garbage disposal is disturbing the protective
snow covering in order to bury food waste. When the temperature drops to zero, such protection saves the worms,
but your garbage also piles up!

Bedding temperatures above 86°F (30°C) could be harmful to the worms. The temperature in moist bedding is generally lower than the surrounding air because evaporation
of moisture from the bedding in a well-ventilated place has
a cooling effect. Locations that could get too hot include a
poorly-ventilated, over-heated attic; outside under a hot sun;
and higher elevations in a greenhouse.

Moisture

All worms need moisture. They "breathe" through their
skin, which must be moist for exchange of air and excretion
of waste to take place. You can add water to dry bedding
when necessary. Too much moisture, present as water standing in the bin, can reduce available oxygen and cause worms
to "drown." This can be a problem in plastic bins, a point I
will discuss in more detail in Chapter 10. Location is another concern with excess moisture. Place your worm bin
where there is no danger of natural flooding, which could
also drown the worms.

Acidity

Redworms can tolerate a fairly wide range of acidity in
their environment, but slightly acid conditions are best. The
14-point scale for determining degree of acidity is called
pH. The most acid reading would be pH1; the most alkaline reading would be pH14. Neutral is pH7, meaning that
the medium is neither acid nor alkaline. A wide range from
pH5 to pH9 is suitable for redworms. In a worm bin with
pH4 , you may find worms dying or trying to escape from
the excessive acidity in their environment. Too much acid
food would be rather like pouring a bottle of vinegar into a
worm bin—not a good idea!

Ventilation

Worms use oxygen in their bodily processes, producing carbon dioxide, just as we do. It is important that you allow air to circulate around your container as a structural unit. Wrapping it in a plastic bag, for example, might be tidy, but the worms would quickly smother.

YOUR NEEDS

To meet your needs, a home vermicomposting system will have to measure up to your expectations, provide a convenient method for converting organic waste to a usable end product, and satisfy your concept of suitable aesthetics. Potential end products are a supply of worms for fishing, worm castings for plants, or vermicompost for use in your garden.

Vermicompost is a more general term than worm castings. A casting is manure, the material deposited from the anus after it's moved through the digestive tract of a worm. Vermicompost contains worm castings, but also consists of partially decomposed bedding and organic waste with recognizable fragments of plants, food, and bedding. Worms of all ages, cocoons, and associated organisms may be found in vermicompost. If a worm bin is left untended for six months or so, worms will eat all of the bedding and organic waste, depositing castings as they do so. In time, they will have reingested the materials a number of times. Then, the entire contents will be fully converted to **vermicast,** which is completely worm worked and re-worked material with a fine smooth texture. Vermicast is considered overworked and has probably lost nutrients. Since no food remains for the worms, most worms will die and be decomposed by the other organisms in the worm bin. The few worms that live will be small, inactive, and undernourished.

The effectiveness of your vermicomposting system will depend partly upon your expectations and partly upon your behavior. You can reasonably expect to bury a large portion of your biodegradable kitchen waste in a properly prepared worm bin, check it occasionally, make judgments about what must be done, then harvest worms and vermicompost or worm castings after a period of several months. You cannot expect to merely dump all the trash from your kitchen into a worm bin, add some worms, and come back in only two weeks to collect quantities of fine, dark worm castings to sprinkle on your house plants. Either revise this unreasonable expectation to something more realistic, perhaps along the ideas below, or don't even begin setting up a system.

Expectations

The difference between what is and what is not reasonable to expect has to do with the kind of material you bury, the environment you provide for the worms, the length of time you are willing to wait to observe changes, and the character of the end products. It isn't that difficult when you know what you want. Guidelines to help you make reasonable judgments about maintaining your worm bin effectively depend on your goals.

Goal: Extra worms
for fishing
Maintenance level: High

Some of you will want to produce more worms than you started with so that you can have a ready supply for fishing. Expect to harvest your bin every two to three months, transfer worms to fresh bedding, and accept vermicompost that is less finished than if you were to leave the worms in their original bedding longer.

Goal: Finished worm castings

for plants

Maintenance level: Low

Those who prefer to obtain castings in the most finished form also have the advantage of extremely low maintenance. You will bury food waste in your worm bin over a four-month period, then leave it alone. You won't have to feed or water the worms for the next few months, while letting the entire culture proceed at its own pace. The worms will produce castings continuously as they eat the bedding and food waste. The disadvantage of this program is that, as the proportion of castings increases, wastes which are toxic to the worms accumulate, and the environment for worms becomes less healthy. They get smaller, stop reproducing, and many die. As you wait for the worms to convert all the bedding and food waste to castings, you will have to deposit fresh batches of food waste elsewhere—perhaps in a compost pile or in a second worm bin.

In time, your worm bin will provide a quantity of fine castings to give you a homogeneous, nutrient-rich potting soil. If you choose this goal, you can alternate from one bin to the other. Or, you may have to purchase worms every fall when you set up your worm bin. This low-maintenance program enables you to vermicompost inside during the cold winter months, compost outside in the traditional manner when the weather warms up, and have finished worm castings from your indoor worm bin sometime during the summer.

A nickname for this maintenance technique might be "lazy person's." However, if you use two bins, it's actually a pretty efficient system; "smart person's" technique fits the situation better.

Goal: Continuous worm supply
plus vermicompost
Maintenance level: Medium

"Middle of the roaders" can opt for a program that requires just enough maintenance to keep the worms healthy. You will harvest fewer worm castings, but you should still have ample quantities of vermicompost to use on your house plants and garden, and enough worms to set up your bin again. About every four months, you will need to prepare fresh bedding and select one of several techniques for separating worms from vermicompost. These techniques are described in Chapter 10.

It should be apparent that the effectiveness of your home vermicomposting system will depend as much upon you as it will depend upon the worms.

Convenience

The convenience of your home vermicomposting system is directly related to its location. There are various possibilities:

Kitchen

Since food preparation is done in the kitchen, the most convenient location for a worm bin might be there, too. One of my friends has a worm bin on top of his dishwasher with

a cutting board serving as a lid. When he is through chopping cabbage, celery, or whatever, he just slides the top back and scrapes the waste into his worm bin. You can't beat that for convenience!

Patio

An outdoor patio off the kitchen is an excellent location for a home vermicomposting unit if it will be out of direct sun during the summer months. It is close to the origin of food waste, close to a water supply for maintaining proper moisture, and it has plenty of ventilation. Just as you can expect to get dirt on the floor when you mix potting soils to repot plants, the periodic maintenance in separat-

ing worms from vermicompost can get messy. Doing it on the patio will also keep the dirt outside. In climates where freezing temperatures are a problem, insulation and supplemental heat can keep the worms going. I describe some of these adaptations in Chapter 10.

Balcony

Apartment-dwellers are often limited for space. In warmer climates, many people living in apartments find that their balcony accommodates a worm bin and a few container plants. They like the appearance of the plants, and feel good about doing something useful with their garbage. The plants give them a place to put the vermicompost produced in the worm bin.

Garage

A well-ventilated garage would be a satisfactory location for a worm bin if it blocks freezing temperatures in your production area. It also will provide shade during hot weather.

Basement

Locating a worm bin in a basement, if you have one, has the advantage of keeping it out of the way. If problems develop—there might be short-term odors or occasional fruit flies—the worm bin is not in the immediate living quarters. You might find it inconvenient to always go downstairs whenever you want to bury garbage, however. Basements do meet the worms' temperature needs, being cooler in summer and rarely freezing in winter. Since they are out of sight and not in the way for most people, many worm bins, including mine, are located in a basement.

Aesthetic considerations

For some of you, locating your worm bin will depend considerably on what it looks like. A homemade bin may be practical, but not necessarily beautiful. If it is a custommade unit of laminated maple with sturdy legs on ball rollers and looks like a piece out of the Nieman-Marcus catalog, you will want it where you can show it off most readily.

Figure 1. Gale Enemark's coffee-table worm bin is in her sitting room.

More realistically, before you decide where to locate your worm bin: 1) determine how large your unit must be to process your kitchen waste; 2) assess the space you have available; and, 3) determine whether you want it to be merely functional and out of the way, or whether you want it to be the center of attention. To put it another way, how many guests do you want tramping through your basement? Or, how many guests can deal with sitting on a window seat worm bin in the dining room? From my experiences, I can guarantee you, until worm bins are common, almost everyone who visits is going to want to see yours!

3.
What container should I use?

A variety of containers make satisfactory worm bins. These range from commercially available vermicomposting units to containers you adapt or bins you build yourself. Regardless of your choice, aeration is an important function of the controlled environment the container must provide. I'll give specific instructions for building a wooden worm bin and describe some of the commercial units later. But first, let's look generally at shape, size, and structural material of possible containers.

GENERAL CONSIDERATIONS

Shape

Because redworms need lots of oxygen, whatever the shape of their bin, their container *must* have holes in the sides, top, or bottom to let air in, but keep the flies out. Sometimes a mesh screen is used to cover the holes. Or a rectangle is cut out of the bottom, side, or lid and covered with screen to provide more opportunity for air to get to the bedding. Various sizes and styles of louvered vents also permit air exchange.

The ideal worm bin is shallow, usually no more than 12-18 inches (30-45cm) deep. The reason for this shallowness is that redworms tend to feed upwards, nibbling from beneath the material on the surface. More surface, more nibbling. Bedding can pack down in a deep container. Such compression pushes the air out of the bottom layers, and consequent development of foul-smelling **anaerobic** conditions is more likely.

In the absence of oxygen, the worms become unhealthy and may die as anaerobic microorganisms break down the waste. These microorganisms live and reproduce only when no oxygen is present. As they break down waste, they produce gases that have foul-smelling, disagreeable odors. You can tell that anaerobes are working when you remove the lid from a smelly garbage can. The secret to having an odor-free worm bin is to have oxygen available throughout the bedding so that both the worms and different kinds of microorganisms can break down the waste aerobically.

The greatest concern that people express when they hear about placing kitchen waste in a container to be kept inside the home, is, "But won't it smell?" The answer is, "Not too badly *if* it is properly set up and maintained."

We are trying to create an **aerobic** environment, one in which oxygen is present throughout the bedding. Oxygen is necessary not only for the worms, but for the millions of aerobic microorganisms that also break down the food waste. As the worms and microorganisms consume the food waste, oxygen from the air combines with carbon in the food waste in a process that releases energy to carry on their work. They give off carbon dioxide and water and other plant nutrients as waste products. The advantage to our senses is that neither carbon dioxide nor water smells.

Given bins of different shapes but equal volume, the one with greater surface area allows more air to contact the bedding and provides more surface on which to place waste. Some commercial units use a system with several layers to support worms and bedding. The worms work from the bottom up through a mesh screen into the layer above. Such stacking units allow the unit to take up less floor space, but still provide much surface area for aeration.

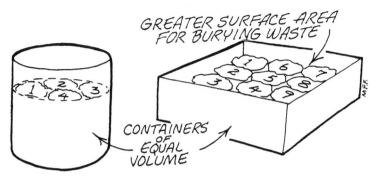

Figure 2. Shallow containers have more surface area for burying waste.

Size

How do you decide how big your home vermicomposting unit should be? First, you need some idea of how much organic kitchen waste you produce. I recommend that you keep track of how many pounds you throw away each week. Is it five pounds? Or ten pounds? Many things affect this. How many individuals do you have in your household? Are you vegetarians who generate more worm food than meat-eaters? How often do you eat out? Do you use prepared mixes or start from scratch? How often do you have to throw away leftovers and spoiled food? The amount of food for worms varies depending on the menu, visitors, and vegetables in season.

Two attitudes affect the volume of waste thrown away: 1) As we become more conscious of how wasteful we are, we tend to be more careful and have less to throw away; 2) We know that whatever waste we do discard will go to good use. The worms will convert it to worm castings, which are then used to grow better vegetables, so we feel less guilty about discarding food waste. I don't know how this contradiction actually influences the volume of waste.

Example 1

My household of two non-vegetarian adults produces about five pounds (2.5 kg) of worm food per week. It consists of such waste as potato peels, citrus rinds, outer leaves of lettuce and cabbage, tea bags or herb tea leaves, moldy leftovers, plate scrapings, cucumber peelings, pulverized egg shells, and onion skins. We often eat lunch at home, and may eat dinner out two or three times a week. Based upon one square foot of surface for each pound of garbage

Plan on one square foot of surface for each pound of garbage per week (one-tenth square meter surface for each half kg)

(one-tenth square meter for each half kilogram) per week, we need a bin with five square feet (one-half square meter) surface area.

Example 2

A one-adult household where the father loves to cook has from 1.75 to 12 pounds (0.8kg to 5.5kg) of waste to feed worms per week. Their average over a 14-week period was 5.2 pounds (2.5kg) per week. He used a 1' x 2' x 3' (30cm x 60cm x 90cm) bin. This size still approximates one square foot surface for each pound of garbage per week (one-tenth sq m for each half kg).

Structural material

Common materials for worm bins are wood and plastic. Wooden bins "breathe" more than plastic, but they deteriorate more quickly because the wood is damp all the time. In dry conditions, the bedding in wooden bins can dry out, so water must be added when needed. Just the wood in a wooden bin is heavy; by the time you add bedding, water, worms, and garbage, it gets very heavy. Moving it is out of the question.

Note: I do not recommend using pressure-treated lumber for worm bin interiors. I am concerned about the chemical compounds used as preservatives which contain copper, chromium, or arsenic **(CCA),** for example. Its use subjects our environment to toxic materials which can be dangerous to people, pets, and water supplies.

Plastic bins require more holes for aeration than wooden bins, and tend to accumulate excess moisture. Plastic containers initially used for other purposes are often readily available, however, and easy to adapt by drilling holes in them. Just remember, whether you purchase a commercial unit or build your own, a closed bin with no provision for aeration will produce as many odors as a closed garbage can, and you'll kill your worms before they even get a chance to eat your garbage.

Caution:

If you want to improvise with containers on hand, be sure that the one you select has not been used to store chemicals, such as pesticides, which may kill the worms. Some worm growers suggest that you scrub new plastic containers with a strong detergent, then rinse them carefully before you grow worms in them.

WOODEN WORM BINS

How long will a wooden box last? Used continuously, without ever letting the box dry out, unfinished wooden boxes should last two to three years. Longevity can be increased by letting the box dry out for several days between setups. Some people rotate between two boxes for more convenient maintenance. A good finish, such as polyurethane varnish, epoxy, or other waterproofing material, that seals all edges should extend box life considerably.

A simple wooden box made of boards, plywood, recycled wood, or an old drawer works as a worm bin if you drill several one-inch (25mm) holes in the sides about two to three inches (5-8cm) from the bottom and then another row along the top of each side. Two very common sizes for wooden worm bins are 1' x 2' x 3' (30cm x 60cm x 90cm) and 2' x 2' x 8" (60cm x 60cm x 20cm). The first of these foot-measured lengths is sometimes called a 1-2-3 bin. It is large enough to handle an average of six to seven pounds (3kg) of garbage per week, or the food waste expected from a family of four to six people. These units require only a hammer and a drill with a one-inch (25mm) bit; constructing larger bins for multiple purposes involves a longer list of appropriate tools.

1-2-3 Worm Box

English Units	#	Items	Metric Units
5/8" x 35 5/8" x 12"	2	pieces CDX plywood	1.5cm x 90cm x 30cm
5/8" x 23 3/8" x 12"	2	pieces CDX plywood	1.5cm x 58.5cm x 30cm
5/8" x 24" x 36"	1	piece CDX plywood	1.5cm x 60cm x 90cm
2" 1 1/2"	38	Ardox nails or screws	5cm 3.7cm

Figure 3. Few materials are needed for a 1-2-3 Worm Box.

Note that the CDX plywood, mentioned in Figure 3 and others, is exterior grade, good one side; #2 pine boards or scrap lumber can be substituted. Ardox nails have a spiral shape which increases their holding power, particularly important for wood which is alternately wet and dry.

Figure 4 shows how to interlock the corners for greater strength. Once the sides are nailed together with about four nails per side, secure the sides to the bottom plywood sheet using five to seven nails per side. Some people will prefer to use self-driving screws with a power drill; screws hold better than nails. Drill six one-inch (2.5cm) holes in each

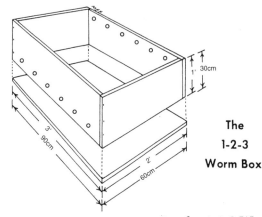

The

1-2-3

Worm Box

Figure 4. Construction diagram for the 1-2-3 Worm Box includes side overlap on corners for strength and holes in sides for aeration.

side, one row along the bottom as shown, and another row along the top. These allow aeration. Having a row along the top of one side permits escape of air if the temperature gets too high in the bin. Interestingly, the worms don't usually crawl out of the holes. Stapling screen over the holes on the inside of the bin will prevent material from falling out, although this step is not critical in most cases.

English Units	#	Items	Metric Units
5/8" x 23 3/8" x 8"	4	pieces CDX plywood	1.5cm x 58.5cm x 20cm
5/8" x 24" x 24"	1	piece CDX plywood	1.5cm x 60cm x 60cm
2" 1 1/2"	36	Ardox nails or screws	5cm 3.7cm

Figure 5. These materials are needed for a Two-Person Bin.

Two-Person Bin

Substitute woods may be used for this bin, too. Nail the sides together, overlapping the corners as shown in Figure 4. Secure the bottom to the sides using about five nails per side. Drill three one-inch (2.5cm) holes about two inches (5cm) from the bottom of two opposite sides for aeration.

Patio Bench Worm Bin

A more elaborate but effective design is the Patio Bench Worm Bin, adapted from a design developed by Seattle Tilth, an urban gardening organization in Washington State. By means of workshops, brochures, and their home composting demonstration site, Tilth volunteers have taught thousands of people how to do worm composting.

The Patio Bench Worm Bin is attractive, serving both as a garbage disposal site and a bench. With a capacity from eight to 16 pounds of food waste (3.5-7kg) per week, it is large enough for most families of four to six people, and can be constructed in nine easy steps. A single sheet of 4' x 8' (120cm x 240cm) exterior grade plywood one-half inch (1.25cm) thick makes up the sides, bottom, and lid. Framing lumber provides structural support so that it is strong

Figure 6. A Patio Bench Bin sits on block supports so that its bottom is two or three inches (5-8cm) above the grass-ground level.

enough to sit upon. Materials will cost between \$35-45 including hardware (hinges, screws, and nails). Wood stain, non-toxic paint, or polyurethane will make it more attrac-

English Units	#	Items	Metric Units
8' 2"x4"	3	construction grade lumber	240cm 36 x 72mm
6' 2"x4"	1	CDX plywood (exterior grade, good one side)	180cm 36 x 72mm
pound	1	4d galvanized nails (to fasten plywood into 2x4 stock)	450g
pound	1/4	8d galvanized nails	115g
pound	1/4	20d galvanized nails (to fasten 2x4 stock together)	115g
3"	2	T-hinges	70mm
1/4" hole	4	screw eyes	60mm hole
8'x3/16"	1	nylon rope length	240cm x 5mm
1"	8	round soffit vents or ventilating louvres	25mm
quart	1	salad oil, poly varnish, wood stain, or marine enamel	750ml
pint	1	appropriate cleanup solvents	375ml

Figure 7. More materials are needed for a Patio Bench Bin.

tive and help seal the wood to make it last longer. Another option for preserving the wood is to coat the wood inside and out with a coat of salad oil.

Tools needed:

> Table saw, circular saw, or rip hand saw
> Hand or power drill with 1" (25mm) bit
> Tape measure, hammer, saw horses, long
>   straight edge, screwdriver
> Wood chisel, wood glue
> Paint brush for application of salad oil, paint,
>   or stain; you can also apply salad oil with
>   a cloth.
> Appropriate solvent for cleanup of wood
>   preservative selected

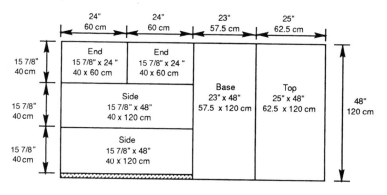

4' x 8' sheet of half-inch plywood
120cm x 240cm x 1.25cm

Figure 8. Cutting pattern for plywood shows little waste.

English Units	#	Worm Bin Parts	Metric Units
15 7/8" x 24"	2	ends	40cm x 60cm
15 7/8" x 48"	2	sides	40cm x 120cm
23" x 48"	1	base	57.5cm x 120cm
25" x 48"	1	lid	62.5cm x 120cm

Figure 9. These dimensions for each worm bin part will result in a Patio Bench Bin, shown in Figures 6 and 13.

Step 1. Cut plywood as shown in Figure 8.

Measure a full 48" (120cm) from the left for the first cut, and make the base a full 23" x 48" (57.5cm x 120cm). Figure 9 summarizes the dimensions of all parts. Width of the saw cuts will make the final measurement less than a full 25" (62.5cm) for the top, but this won't matter.

Step 2. Cut framing lumber as shown in Figure 10.

One 8' board
48"	48"

Two 8' boards
51"	25"	20"

One 6' board
13"	13"	13"	20"

Figure 10. This cutting diagram uses all framing lumber.

English Units	#	Worm Bin Part	Metric Units
48"	2	base sides	120.0cm
20"	3	base ends and center	50.0cm
51"	2	lid sides	127.5cm
25"	2	lid ends	62.5cm
13"	4	corner supports	32.5cm

Figure 11. Board lengths of each worm bin part vary in the Patio Bench.

Step 3. Assemble the base.

Place the base sides on edge. Use two 3 1/2 " (90mm) screws or two 4" (10cm, 20d,) nails to secure the base sides

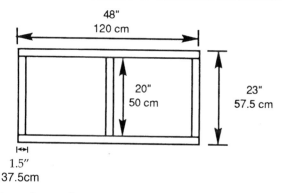

Figure 12. Base frame has all 2x4's on edge.

to the ends and center spacers as in Figure 12. Short pieces go **inside**! Then fasten the 23"x48" (57.5 x 120cm) plywood to the base. This sheet will be the floor of your worm bin.

Step 4. Secure corner supports to sides.

Place two corner supports flatside down on large flat surface. Lay a 15"x48" (37.5cm x 120cm) sidepiece on corner supports, line up top and side edges, and fasten plywood to each corner support with three or four 1 1/2" (38mm) screws or nails. Repeat for second side.

Step 5. Fasten ends to sides to make the box.

With a helper, place sides against the base and secure the plywood ends to the side panels, screwing or nailing into the corner supports. These supports provide a solid surface for fastening and strengthening the box. Note that the side panels do not extend all the way to the ground. This helps to prevent moisture from seeping up into the edges of the plywood from the ground. Screw or nail the box around the base, using a fastener every three to four inches (8 to 10cm).

Step 6. Drill ventilation holes in side panels.

Drill four to eight 1" (25mm) holes about 3" (75mm) from the floor on one side of the bin. Drill a similar number of holes about 3" (75mm) from the top of the other side of the bin to help in ventilation. Warm air can exit from the top, drawing cooler air in from the bottom. Installation of ventilation louvres (soffit vents) in these holes after painting will dress up the appearance of the bin and help keep insects or rodents from entering.

Step 7 (for those working with English units).

Assemble the lid. The plywood lid is supported by a 2"x4" frame with lap joints in the corners. To make the lap joints, set your saw to cut 3/4" deep, which is half the thickness of a 2x4. Taking the 51" long and 25" long boards, measure 3 1/2" from each end. Make shallow cuts every half-inch up to the 3 1/2-inch mark. Then, use a sharp wood chisel to knock out the extra wood. Be consistent in which half of each end is cut out, e.g., you may cut the top half out of the ends, the bottom half out of the sides. Repeat this eight times, once for each end of the four boards. Glue and secure the lap joints together with 4d nails or 1 1/2" screws. Once the glue has set, center the 25"x48" plywood lid on the frame and fasten it with 1 1/2" fasteners every six inches.

Step 7 (for those working with metric units).

Assemble the lid. The plywood lid is supported by a frame made of 36mm x 72mm framing lumber with lap joints in the corners. To make the lap joints, set your saw to cut 18mm deep, which is half the thickness of a 36x72 board. Taking the 127.5cm long and 62.5cm long boards, measure 88mm from each end. Make shallow cuts every 10mm up to the 88mm mark. Then, use a sharp wood chisel to knock out the extra wood. Be consistent in which half of each end is cut out, e.g., you may cut the top half out of the ends, the bottom half out of the sides. Repeat this eight times, once for each end of the four boards. Glue and secure the lap joints together with 4d nails or 37.5mm screws. Once the glue has set, center the 62.5 x 120cm plywood lid on the frame and fasten it with 37.5mm fasteners every150mm.

Step 8. Apply the hinges.

Place the T-hinge so that the screws for the strap will insert into the corner supports. The rectangular part of the hinge should be vertical while the lid is up. Attach hinges with screws after drilling pilot holes.

Step 9. Provide lid support.

Use nylon rope to keep the lid from falling backwards and reduce strain on the hinges. Nylon will last longer without deterioration than ropes made of natural fibers such as cotton or hemp. To secure the rope, attach screw eyes in corners of lid and at front inside edges of the box. Knot the rope to hold it in place at an appropriate length.

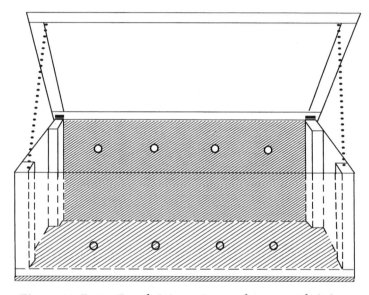

Figure 13. Patio Bench Worm Bin is shown with lid up.

Indoor furniture

Some people have built worm bins as pieces of furniture, providing legs on casters, staining and finishing boards of finer grades of wood, or using a more attractive (and more expensive) grade of plywood, such as birch. You should be aware of two precautions: use exterior grade plywood, and avoid highly aromatic woods. Since the box will be damp most of the time, you don't want the composite wooden layers of the plywood sheet to separate from each other. At one time I believed that all aromatic woods, such as redwood and cedar, might be harmful to worms. Worm workers from "Redwood Country" tell me that redwood works just fine for worm bins. The jury is still out on cedar.

PLASTIC WORM BINS

Not everyone wants to build their own worm bins. They may not have the tools, the time, or a pickup truck to bring a 4'x8' (120 cm x 240 cm) sheet of plywood home from the lumber yard to construct a wooden worm bin.   Sufficient interest exists in vermicomposting that a number of companies now produce various models of vermicomposting bins. I will point out some of the features of several worm bins currently on the market.

The Original Vermicomposter
The first home vermicomposting unit available commercially in North America was Al Eggan's Original Vermicomposter produced in Toronto, Canada. This lidded plastic bin has holes in the bottom for drainage and sits on rubber foot supports on a drainage tray. Several small vents in the lid provide some ventilation.

Gardener's Supply Worm Bin
This plastic bin available from a Vermont mail-order vendor is 24"x 20" x11" (60 x 50 x 27.5cm). The bin has solid sides with a decorative mesh for the bottom. The mesh openings allow some aeration and permit excess water to drain onto the second lid which serves as a tray. A foam filter on top of the mesh bottom supports bedding and worms which can be purchased separately.

Can-O-Worms™
The home vermicomposting unit which has achieved most commercial success is undoubtedly the rectangular RELN Worm Factory marketed in Australia and its circular counterpart known as the Can-O-Worms in New Zealand,

Canada, and the United States. Designed with a completely enclosed tiered system, the bottom catchment tray has a spigot for draining excess water, sometimes called "vermi-compost tea." Three working trays with mesh bottoms sit one on top of the other upon the base unit that has legs keeping all raised up from the floor. This gives room for a bucket to collect the liquid. The homeowner places moist coconut fiber bedding and a starting population of composting worms on the first mesh tray. Food waste is added to this tray. When the first tray is full, food waste is added to the second mesh tray. The worms find their way up to the food in this level and begin processing this food waste, depositing their castings in the lower level. With several tiers to

Figure 14. Two of the four tiers of the circular Can-O-Worms bin are shown above.

move up and fresh food as an incentive, worms are supposed to vacate the bottom level which eventually contains finely processed worm castings. These are readily removed by hand or simply flushed through the system with a garden hose, depending on the homeowner's preference. With over 130,000 of the RELN units sold, an estimated 11,000 tons per year of food waste are being diverted from centralized systems for pickup, transport, and processing or landfilling.

Worm-a-way®

The patented Worm-a-way®, manufactured in two sizes by Flowerfield Enterprises, is an aerated plastic bin made of recycled plastic. Ventilation louvres support perforated pipes which traverse the lower part of the bin. This assembly is designed to enhance aeration in the lower part of the bin, almost always a problem with plastic bins. Large vents in the lid provide additional opportunity for air exchange.

Figure 15. Worm-a-way bins feature transverse ventilation pipes near the base.

Recommended bedding is shredded newspaper because anyone can get it at no cost. The larger size (20"x 24"x 12", 50 x 60 x 30cm) can handle about five pounds (>2kg) of food waste per week. Waste processing capacity of the smaller Worm-a-way is about two to three pounds (1-1.5kg) of garbage per week. Flowerfield generally recommends that re-

cycling coordinators and others who need to carry a demonstration bin around with them use the smaller size
(16"x19"x13", 40x48x33cm). After adding several weeks'
worth of food scraps to the container containing moistened bedding, soil, and worms, the smaller container easily
weighs 35 or 40 pounds (15-20kg).

Variations of the bins described above provide such
things as spigots for drainage; footies or legs to support the
bin off the floor and elevate bottom drainage holes; false
bottoms so that excess water can pass through to the bottom level rather than making the bedding soggy; and, every pattern of drilled holes that creative minds can imagine. Many people purchase plastic storage containers from
discount stores, drill holes in the bottom, sides, and/or tops,
and make worm bins that work just fine for them.

The perfect worm bin has yet to be designed. Fortunately many designs work, provided they are well-aerated,
well-drained, and not subject to extreme temperatures.

4.
What are worm beddings?

A major component of your home vermicomposting system is bedding. Worm beddings are multi-functional since they not only hold moisture, but provide a medium in which the worms can work, as well as a place to bury the garbage. Worm bedding is usually some form of cellulose, a carbon source which provides energy to the organisms which break it down. Since worms will eventually consume the bedding as well as the garbage, bedding must not be toxic to the worms. The most desirable beddings are also light and fluffy, the two conditions necessary for air ex-

change throughout the depth of the container. This exchange helps control offensive odors by reducing the chances that anaerobic conditions will develop.

If left six months or more, all the bedding may be converted to vermicast. It can become so dense that the worms have a hard time moving through it. When this material is partially dried and then screened, it is impossible to identify either bedding or the garbage that was originally buried. However, normal procedures for maintaining a healthy worm population (discussed in Chapter 10), require that worms be removed from the bedding while it is still vermicompost, prior to complete conversion to vermicast.

Many materials make satisfactory beddings. Mixtures may be used, but a few cautions apply. Some of the more common beddings are listed below, along with brief comments on their advantages and disadvantages. Your choice can be highly individual, depending upon availability, convenience, and economic considerations.

BEDDING MATERIALS

Hand-shredded newsprint

The least expensive and most readily available bedding is newspaper strips you shred by hand. By fully opening a section of newspaper, tearing it lengthwise down the centerfold, gathering the two halves, tearing it lengthwise again, and repeating the process five to six times for each section, you will get strips ranging from one to three inches (25mm-75mm) wide. It doesn't take long to fill your bin with bedding and accumulate enough in a large plastic bag to change the bedding in a few months

ADVANTAGES
- No cost
- Readily available
- Odorless
- No dust

DISADVANTAGES
- Requires preparation time
- Inked newsprint can be dirty to handle
- Large strips dry out more readily than machine-shredded paper
- Tends to mat into layers, making it difficult to bury garbage

The most commonly asked question about newsprint is, "Isn't the newspaper ink harmful to the worms?" No, as long as we limit the question to black ink. The basic ingredients of black ink are carbon black and oils, neither of which is toxic to worms. With increasing numbers of newspapers using soy inks, the oils are even of less concern.

Colored inks, however, may be a problem. At one time heavy metals, such as lead, barium, chromium, and cadmium, were major components of their pigments. Government regulations and increasing environmental awareness of these substances' toxicity greatly reduced the use of heavy metals in pigments. When I burn a newspaper insert in my fireplace and the flames turn beautiful blue and green colors, they tell me some heavy metals are still present. Since enough black ink and lightly colored newsprint is available, I try to avoid using heavily colored advertising sections in my worm bin.

Machine-shredded newsprint or computer strips

Paper-shredding machines produce high volumes of good worm bedding from both newsprint and computer print-out paper. The long, tangled lengths of quarter-inch (6mm) wide strips are easily moistened. Computer paper strips don't hold moisture quite as well as the newspaper because the paper has a harder surface. The worms will eventually eat the softened paper, however, so the end result will also be worm castings.

Where can you get paper that is shredded? Look and ask around. Banks and universities frequently shred volumes of computer records; many offices have paper shredders. One hobbicraft business bought a machine to shred newspapers so that its customers would have packing for their greenware and finished ceramic pieces. You only need a supply for use a few times during the year.

ADVANTAGES
- Clean
- Usually free
  for the hauling
- Odorless
- Easily prepared

DISADVANTAGES
- May be hard to find
- Harder to moisten than
  newsprint
- Recycling the fiber may
  be a higher use than
  worm bedding

Leaf mold

The bottom of a pile of decaying leaves can yield a satisfactory bedding in the form of partially decomposed leaves. If they are wet, you'll probably even find some worms! Maple leaves are preferable to oak, which take a long time to break down.

ADVANTAGES
- No cost
- Natural worm habitat

DISADVANTAGES
- Unwanted organisms may be present
- Leaves can mat together, making it difficult to bury garbage

Animal manures

Composted horse, rabbit, or cow manures are good bedding for worms. Manure is a natural habitat for them, but may be difficult to obtain. It should not come from recently wormed animals because the drugs used to kill parasitic worms may kill your redworms as well. Some people may object to the initial odor, although that will disappear within a few days after redworms are added. Manure is likely to have other organisms such as mites, sowbugs, centipedes, or grubs, which some people would rather not have in their homes if they can help it.

Setting up a bin with manure is a two-stage process, since the medium may heat up beyond the tolerance of worms when water is added. However, the redworms can be added in about two days when it cools down. A forkful of moistened manure can be placed on top of other bedding periodically to help revive a waning culture. Worms will invade the mass and thrive on the nutrients available.

ADVANTAGES
- Can be free for the hauling
- Natural worm habitat
- Variety of nutrients present
- Makes good castings

DISADVANTAGES
- May not be readily available
- Initial odors can be objectionable
- Unwanted organisms may be present
- May initially heat up, delaying time when worms can be added
- Can compact easily

Coconut fiber

Sometimes known as coir, coconut fiber is a clean, easy-to-prepare worm bedding that is becoming more popular as it becomes more available. It comes to market as a block of compressed fiber which expands rapidly when placed in the appropriate volume of water. The moistened fiber is then placed in the worm bin where the worms seem to thrive in it. Less acidic than peat moss (pH5 compared with pH3.9), coir has high water-holding capacity, and is not supposed to decompose as fast as peat. One woman noted, however, that the worms liked the coir so well they didn't go after the food she was burying in her worm bin! Coir can be effectively mixed with any of the other beddings described to aid water retention or to make manure beddings less dense. I recommend using one-third to one-half coir with other bedding.

Much of the coir is a waste product of the Sri Lankan coconut industry, and large accumulations of this natural fiber present disposal problems on the island. Exporting it as a substitute for peat moss helps reduce waste disposal problems, provides much-needed income, and helps save the limited resource which peat moss represents. Coir is fairly expensive, primarily due to the high transportation costs to the distributor, the retailer, and to the end-user, so its use in worm bins is not totally environmentally benign.

ADVANTAGES		DISADVANTAGES
•Retains moisture well		•Must be purchased
•Clean		•High transportation costs
•Odorless		
•Good for mixing with other beddings		

Wood chips

Worm bin users report that hardwood chips make excellent worm bedding. Mixed with leaves or other bedding materials capable of holding moisture, wood chips provide bulk and create air spaces throughout the bedding. Unlike other beddings which are consumed by the worms and become vermicompost, wood chips can be reused by screening them when vermicompost is harvested from the bin.

ADVANTAGES
- Clean
- Odorless
- Maintain aerobic
  conditions in bin
- Good for mixing with
  other beddings
- Can be reused

DISADVANTAGES
- Dry out readily
- Availability limited
  to those with
  chipper/shredders

Peat moss

Whether from Canada or Tasmania and despite its acidity, sphagnum peat moss has been a standard bedding among some commercial worm growers. It remains the most common medium for shipping worms. Because it is a nonrenewable resource and widely recognized as being environmentally and commercially unsustainable, I no longer recommend its use as worm bedding.

ADDITIONS TO BEDDING

Soil

You may have noticed that I have not mentioned using dirt or soil for bedding. In nature, redworms are litter dwellers; that is, they are found among masses of decaying vegetation such as fallen leaves or manure piles, or under rotten logs. Redworms are present in mineral soils only when large amounts of organic materials are also present. Although one investigator recommends using a thin (1/2", 1cm) layer of soil in a container holding worms, I have not found that quantity to be essential for home vermicomposting systems. In fact, a big disadvantage of soil is its weight. With just a half-inch of soil, for example, a container is extremely heavy. I do recommend, however, adding a handful or two of soil when initially preparing the bedding. This provides some **grit** to aid in breaking down food particles within the worm's gizzard. It also introduces an inoculum of a variety of soil bacteria, protozoa, and fungi which will aid in the composting process.

Calcium carbonate

Powdered limestone (calcium carbonate) can also be used to provide grit. It has the further advantages of helping to keep conditions in the bin from becoming too acidic, and providing calcium, which is necessary for worm reproduction and survival. You could use the kind that can be mixed with feed or used to line athletic fields, but pulverized egg shells serve the same purpose. Since I add them regularly, I frequently don't bother with the limestone.

Caution:

Do not use slaked, or hydrated lime. The wrong kind of lime will cause your worms to react violently and will kill them.

Rock dust

I highly recommend rock dust as another source of grit. Also called rock powder or rock flour, this is finely ground rock from natural or industrial processes. Natural processes include the grinding of glaciers against rock surfaces to

pulverize the rock, forming sand and silt as a consequence of this erosion. Industrial processes would be gravel-crushing operations to produce aggregate for the construction industry, resulting in a powdery by-product called fines. Depending upon the source rock, rock dust can contain many trace minerals which support plant growth. Combined with the action of microorganisms in a worm bin, the availability of minerals in rock dust enhances plant growth even more effectively than if the rock dust were not present in the vermicompost at all.

Zeolite

Zeolite is a mineral used in granular or powder form in commercial worm beds in Australia and New Zealand to balance pH and absorb ammonia and other odors. Of volcanic origin, zeolite's natural negative charge attracts positively-charged odor molecules and absorbs them on its surface. Using zeolite in a worm bin would provide grit for the worms' gizzards in addition to these other benefits. Although not well-known in the United States, zeolite can be purchased via mail or phone order and from some stores, known as **"green" businesses**, that market environmentally friendly products. They sell it in mesh bags for all-purpose odor control and for alleviation of some so-called environmental illnesses in chemically-sensitive individuals.

5.
What kind of worms
should I use?

Most people think that "a worm is a worm is a worm."
In fact, there are many kinds of worms and they have different jobs to do. It is important to use the right kind of
worms in your home vermicomposting system. You want
a kind of worm that processes large amounts of organic
material. The worms should reproduce quickly in confinement and tolerate the disturbance caused when you lift the
lid to bury food waste or add bedding. When small organisms are raised in a controlled environment, they are said to
be cultured; the culture of earthworms is known as
vermiculture.

Most of the worms that you could dig up from your
garden would not be suitable for vermicomposting. The
soil-dwelling species, or "earthworkers," don't process large
amounts of organic material like the "composters." They
don't reproduce well in confinement, and they won't thrive
in a worm bin if you dig around and mess up their burrow
system. Understanding some things about different kinds
of worms and why common names can be confusing is the
purpose of this chapter.

Redworms are the most satisfactory kind to use in your
home vermicomposting system, but what I call "redworm,"
you may know as "red wiggler." Your neighbor may call it
"manure worm." The bait dealer down the road may refer
to it as "red hybrid." Other common names for this same
animal are fish worm, dung worm, fecal worm, English red
worm, striped worm, stink worm, brandling, and apple
pomace worm. A distinct pattern of alternating red and
buff stripes characterizes some of these worms, hence an-

other common name, "tiger worms." Calling earthworms by common names can cause communication problems. With so many names, how can any of us know when we are talking about the same worm?

SCIENTIFIC NAMES

To be certain they are talking about the same thing, scientists have developed a precise system for naming organisms. Since much information in this book comes from scientific papers, I will be using scientific names. So that you won't be confused when I do, here are some basic rules that all scientists follow:

- The name of each organism consists of two words, the first of which is called a **genus** (plural: **genera***)*; the second, the **species**. All organisms of the same genus are more closely related than those of different genera. Human beings are members of the species *Homo sapiens*.

- Correct usage requires that the genus name always be capitalized and the species name be lower case.

- Both terms are either Latin or Greek in origin. Sometimes they are Latinized versions of words in other languages. Scientific names are italicized in print, or if typewritten, underlined.

Composting worms
Eisenia fetida
The redworms I use are *Eisenia fetida* (which I pronounce, "i SEE nee a FET id a"), said by some to have a fetid odor. An older spelling was *Eisenia foetida*. These worms process large amounts of organic material in their natural

habitats of manure, compost piles, or decaying leaves. They are fast reproducers and tolerate a wide range of temperatures, acidity, and moisture conditions. They are tough worms and withstand handling well. Because sufficient markets exist encouraging people to culture *E. fetida* on a part- or full-time basis, anyone may purchase them almost any season of the year. They can readily be shipped via package delivery services or through the mail.

Eisenia andrei

Eisenia andrei is a close relative which lacks the buff and red striping of the tiger worm. Called the "red tiger," *E. andrei* (abbreviating the genus name to just its initial saves space once it has already been spelled out in full) has the same performance characteristics as *E. fetida*. Most commercial cultures contain a mixture of both species, and growers do not separate them.

Lumbricus rubellus

Lumbricus rubellus is another worm suitable for worm composting. Some consider *L. rubellus* to be the "true" redworm; others call it the dung worm or the red marsh

Figure 16. "Composters" live and work on the surface in upper organic layers of soil. The soil-dwelling "earthworkers" move from one layer to another, mixing layers as they do.

worm. It has been found in compost heaps and manure piles, and in pastures, particularly under cow patties or manure. Because it can be found living in soil rich in organic material, *L. rubellus* probably has potential for doing double-duty as a vermicomposter and as an earthworker.

Many people who vermicompost would like to transfer extra worms from their bins to their gardens in order to increase the worm populations there. I support the idea in concept, but I never recommend this for *E. fetida* because they are not soil-dwellers; with *L. rubellus*, however, it should work. *L. rubellus* looks similar to a nightcrawler but is smaller. The top anterior of the worm is purple-maroon, and it is lighter at the tail and underneath. It tends to be thicker-bodied between the clitellum and the head than other worms. Some worm growers claim to have *L. rubellus* in their beds, but scientists tell me that every time they have checked out the claims, the worms have been *E. fetida, E. andrei,* or a mixture of both species.

Perionyx excavatus

Perionyx excavatus is suitable for vermicomposting in warm climates. Called the Indian blue worm in some regions, it is a tropical species which reproduces well in culture and tolerates handling. Scientific investigations show that *P. excavatus* is intolerant of cold, so it would not live outside through the winter in a cold climate. It also has a tendency to to move out of worm bins for no apparent reason, a characteristic my staff acknowledges by calling them "travelers."

Eudrilus eugeniae

Another restless worm used for vermicomposting, *Eudrilus eugeniae,* is large and commonly known as the African nightcrawler. As its common name suggests, this species has a tropical origin. They can reproduce quickly and can process large amounts of organic material rapidly within their optimal temperature range of 59-77°F (15-25°C); temperatures below 50°F (10°C) kill them. *E. eugeniae* is therefore limited to warm climates or heated buildings.

Earthworkers

Lumbricus terrestris

Most people recognize the nightcrawler, known to some as the dew worm, night walker, rain worm, angle worm, orchard worm, or even night lion. Scientists call it *Lumbricus terrestris*, and it is unquestionably the most studied of the 4400 species of earthworms currently named. One bibliography of earthworm research lists over 200 scientific studies with data on *Lumbricus terrestris!* They are widespread in Europe and North America and are found in parts of New Zealand, but have not been recorded from Australia.

Nightcrawlers are not suitable worms for the type of home vermicomposting system described here. I once placed 80 nightcrawlers in my worm bin along with the redworms already there. Two months later, I found only one live nightcrawler, and it was immature. Although satisfactory environments can be created for nightcrawlers indoors, they require large amounts of soil, and the bed temperature cannot exceed 50°F (10°C). Indoors, your box temperature is likely to get higher than that. Nightcrawlers dig burrows and don't like to have their burrows disturbed. If you try to bury garbage, nightcrawlers move quickly around the surface of the box trying to escape your digging.

Nightcrawlers do play important roles in soil fertility. These large soil-dwelling earthworms have extensive burrows extending from the ground surface to several feet deep. They come to the surface on moist spring and fall nights and forage for food, drawing dead leaves, grass, and other organic material into their burrows where they feed upon it at a later time. Nightcrawlers perform important soil mixing functions. They take organic material into deeper layers of the soil, mix it with subsoils that they consume in their burrowing activities, and bring mineral subsoils to the surface when they deposit their casts. Through their burrows, nightcrawlers also aid in soil aeration and in water retention by increasing the rate at which water can penetrate the deeper soil layers. They may not be good for your worm boxes, but they are very good for your gardens.

Other soil-dwelling species in North America
Except for *L. terrestris* and *L. rubellus,* you would most likely find different worms from those described above if you dig in your garden. In the northern United States and southern parts of Canada, about 90% of the worms found would be one of eight soil-dwelling species, including *Aporrectodea turgida, A. trapezoides, A. tuberculata, Dendrobaena octaedra, Dendrodrilus rubidus, L. terrestris, L. rubellus,* and *Octolasion tyrteum.* More species will be found in the southern part of the United States which was not covered by glaciers 10,000 years ago.

Identifying these species would require suitable magnification, a good pair of forceps, and a tool for pointing or probing. Depending on the guide or identification key you use, preliminary determinations of species can be made on the basis of pigmentation, general body shape, length of the worm, and position of the clitellum. You may have to identify the type of projection over the mouth, locate the position of various openings for sexual organs, and determine the pattern for setae (bristles) on each segment. We need more people who can identify kinds of worms. I encourage more people to learn how to do so.

COMMERCIAL NAMES

A marketing strategy for some worm growers is to create a name that establishes their worms as unique or better than others, so they can justify a higher price. Such names as "Jumbo Worm" or "Super Giant" come to mind. These are probably not different species, and certainly not **hybrids** (combinations of species), but are likely to be just well-fed worms. If you are just buying some worms for fishing, it probably doesn't matter.

But if you are going to use the worms you buy to set up a worm composting system, make sure the grower can give you the scientific name. That way can you be sure that the worm you purchase is suitable for composting and, if you need to learn more about it, you can read some of the scientific papers about your particular worm of choice.

6.
What is the sex life
of a worm?

Before determining how many redworms you need to start vermicomposting, an understanding of their amazing reproductive potential is helpful. Two of the reasons for using redworms are that they reproduce quickly and in culture. When some people learn how fast redworms reproduce, they become concerned that redworms will "take over the world," but their numbers are controlled by environmental factors.

Many people know that a single earthworm is both male and female. However, they may wonder why mating is even necessary when each worm produces both eggs and sperm. Knowledge of a worm's structure helps explain this.

SEX ORGANS AND FUNCTIONS

Mating

The swollen region about one-third of the distance between the head and tail of a worm is the **clitellum**, sometimes known as the girdle, band, or saddle. The presence of a clitellum indicates that a worm is sexually mature. Bait worms with this structure are commonly called "banded breeders," showing that they are old enough to breed and produce offspring. Just as worm species differ in external characteristics, they differ somewhat in mating behavior.

For example, nightcrawlers extend themselves from their burrows to seek another nightcrawler with which to mate. Attracted by glandular secretions, they find each other and lie with their heads in opposite directions, their bodies closely joined. Their clitella secrete large quantities of mucus that forms a tube around each worm. Sperm from each worm move down a groove into receiving pouches of the other worm. The sperm, in a seminal fluid, enter the opening of **sperm storage sacs** where they are held for some time.

Redworms differ from nightcrawlers by mating at different levels in their bedding, rather than just upon the surface. Under proper conditions, they can also be observed mating at any time of year, whereas some species mate only during particular seasons.

Some time after the worms separate, the clitellum secretes a second substance, a material containing albumin. The albuminous material hardens on the outside to form a **cocoon** in which eggs are fertilized and from which baby worms hatch. As the adult worm backs out of this hardening band, it deposits eggs from its own body and the stored sperm from its mate which can fertilize eggs for several cocoons. Sperm fertilize the eggs inside this structure, which closes off at each end as it passes over the first segment. Sometimes called an **egg case**, or capsule, this home for developing worms is more properly called a cocoon.

Cocoons

About the size of a matchhead or a small grain of rice, cocoons are lemon-shaped objects. They change color as the baby worms develop, starting as a luminescent pearly white, becoming quite yellow, then light brown. When the **hatchlings** are nearly ready to emerge, cocoons are reddish. By observing carefully with a good hand lens, it is sometimes possible to see not only a baby worm, but the pumping of its bright red blood vessel. The blood of a worm is amazingly similar to ours, having the same iron-rich hemoglobin as its base to carry oxygen.

It takes at least three weeks development in the cocoon before one to several baby worms hatch. The time to hatch-

EARTHWORM MATING AND COCOON FORMATION

EACH WORM HAS <u>BOTH</u> **OVARIES** AND **TESTES.**

TWO WORMS JOIN BY MUCUS FROM THEIR CLITELLA. SPERM THEN PASS FROM EACH WORM TO THE **SPERM STORAGE SACS** IN THE OTHER WORM.

LATER, A **COCOON** FORMS ON THE CLITELLUM OF EACH WORM. THE WORM BACKS OUT OF THE HARDENING COCOON.

EGGS AND SPERM ARE DEPOSITED IN THE COCOON AS IT PASSES OVER OPENINGS FROM OVARIES AND SPERM STORAGE SACS.

AFTER BEING RELEASED FROM THE WORM, THE COCOON CLOSES AT BOTH ENDS. EGG FERTILIZATION TAKES PLACE IN THE COCOON.

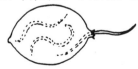

TWO OR MORE BABY WORMS HATCH FROM ONE END OF THE COCOON.

MSF.

Figure 17. Worms are **hermaphroditic.**

ing is highly dependent upon temperature and other conditions. I worked with worms for years before I ever saw a worm emerge from its cocoon. I have observed hatchlings work their way out of their cocoon, thrashing about vigorously. When I turned on bright lights to try to photograph them, they quickly retreated, reacting negatively to light just as adult worms do. I have since been able to videotape baby worms twisting and turning inside their cocoons. Imagine how excited I was to capture on videotape an hour-long sequence of four baby worms hatching from their cocoon!

Newly emerged worms are whitish and nearly transparent, although the blood vessel causes a pink tinge. They may be from one-half to nearly an inch (12mm-25mm) long when they hatch, but they weigh only two to three milligrams. At that size, it would take over 150,000 hatchlings to make one pound (450g) of worms.

Although each cocoon may contain as many as 10 fertilized eggs, normally only two to three hatchlings emerge. The number of hatchlings varies depending upon such factors as the age of the breeder which deposited the cocoon, its nutritional state, the temperature, and whether the temperature is constant or fluctuates daily. This knowledge makes it possible to establish conditions for greater hatchling production.

Maturity

The time it takes for a baby worm to become a breeder varies, depending on the same factors—temperature, moisture, food availability, and population density. A redworm can be sexually mature and produce cocoons in eight weeks, but ten is more common. Once it breeds and begins laying cocoons, it can deposit two to three cocoons per week for six months to a year. Conservatively, then, if a two-month-old breeder laid two cocoons a week for 24 weeks, and two hatchlings emerged from each cocoon, one breeder would produce 96 baby worms in six months (2 cocoons x 24 weeks x 2 hatchlings).

The situation is more complicated than that, however. Before the first two months are up, the first hatchlings will be able to breed. These could produce two cocoons for 16 weeks with two hatchlings coming from each of the four worms resulting from the original breeder's first week's production. Some of the 256 more worms produced during this time will die before the six-month period is up. The math quickly gets complicated, but since optimal conditions for such geometric increases in numbers will never be achieved, theoretical projections are more confusing than informative.

Educated guesses are part of science. As you care for your worms, you will be using your experience to help analyze problems that may crop up. Calculations may be straightforward, but they may depend on assumptions which are probable. For example, consider the potential number of worms you can hope to expect from your bin. Dr. Roy Hartenstein of Syracuse, New York, has calculated that eight individuals could produce about 1500 offspring within six months time. He based this upon their producing two cocoons per worm per week, of which 82% hatch and average 1.5 hatchlings per cocoon. If they reach maturity at five to six weeks and continue producing cocoons for 40 to 50 weeks of fertility at 77°F (25°C), his calculated total would result. Calculations based upon other assumptions would result in different projections.

POPULATION CONTROLS

With the reproductive potential described, we come back to the question of why worms don't take over the world. Three basic conditions control the size of a worm population: 1) availability of food; 2) space requirements; and 3) fouling of their environment.

When food waste is fed regularly to worms in a limited space, the worms and associated organisms, both microscopic and larger, break down this waste. They use what they can and excrete the rest. As the worms reproduce, the voracious young worms compete with their parents and all the other worms in the culture for the limited food available. Additionally, all the worms excrete wastes in their castings which have been shown to be toxic to members of their own species. As time goes on, more worms compete for the limited food, and more and more of the bedding becomes converted to castings. The density of the worms may exceed that favorable for cocoon production, and reproduction slows down. Undesirable conditions in their continually changing environment may cause some worms to die. Some worms will die of old age. Interestingly, you will rarely see dead worms because they are rapidly decomposed by other associated creatures in this active composting environment.

The controls you exert over your worm population will affect this whole process. You may choose to feed an ever-increasing population more and more food. If you want more and more worms, you will eventually have to provide them more space and fresh bedding, and enable them to get away from high concentrations of their castings. You may even choose to become a worm grower, and try to keep up with the ever-increasing demands for food, space, and timely elimination of accumulated end products. But that's another story, and it's more complicated than simply keeping enough worms alive to process your kitchen waste so that you can use the rich end product to grow healthier vegetables and house plants.

7.
How many worms do I need?

Quantities of worms are specified in terms of weight rather than numbers for a couple of reasons, one personal and the other biological. The personal reason is that the first season I sold worms, my partner and I sorted and counted 50,000 worms—one by one by one. If you ever have to count 50,000 of anything one by one, you'll find an easier way to do it, too. From that time on, I have sold worms by weight. Of course, the first question I get is always, "How many worms are in a pound?" Although the number will vary depending upon the size of the worms, there are some guidelines.

Worm growers commonly estimate that there are about 1000 breeders per pound (2200kg) for young redworms. A bait dealer selling worms for fishing would prefer that the worms be considerably larger than that. If redworms don't run between 600 to 700 per pound (1300-1500/kg), customers complain that they are too small to get on a hook.

Biologically, it is the **biomass** of worms, not their number, that is important in vermicomposting. Biomass in this case is the weight of the worms within the worm bin. Worms can consume more than their weight each day, regardless of their size. During their rapid growth stage, juveniles eat proportionally more than adults. Think of feeding a teenager in your home. Since many small worms can move as much material through their intestines as fewer large worms of equal mass, what you want is an earthworm biomass sufficient to do the job.

With some idea of how fast redworms reproduce, you might conclude that your worm bin would eventually produce enough worms to handle all your food waste regardless of how many worms you used initially. You could start with a few dozen redworms and regularly feed them small amounts of garbage. If patience is one of your virtues, you could wait until their natural tendency to reproduce under proper conditions yields several thousand worms. However, most of you will want your worm composting system to handle enough of your organic kitchen waste from the day you set it up to assure yourself that it really works. As the worm population increases, you will be able to add more garbage.

Three factors influence the number of worms you will want to start with:

1) average amount of food waste to be buried per day
2) size of bin, and
3) cost of worms and amount of money you want to spend.

Since your bin size will be based upon how much garbage you expect, the amount you will be burying is really the critical factor. I usually recommend starting with at least a pound (0.5kg) of worms.

Worm to daily garbage ratio

The relationship between weight of worms required and a given amount of garbage can be expressed as "worm:garbage ratio" (the symbol : here means "to"). I recommend a worm:garbage ratio of 2:1, based upon the initial weight of worms and the average daily amount of garbage to be buried. Thus, if you generate seven pounds of garbage per week, you would average one pound of garbage per day (3.2kg per week, or about one-half kg per day):

$$\text{\textit{English units}} \quad \frac{7 \text{ lb garbage/week}}{7 \text{ days in one week}} \quad = \quad \frac{1 \text{ lb garbage/day}}{\text{average}}$$

$$\text{\textit{Metric units}} \quad \frac{3.2\text{kg garbage/week}}{7 \text{ days in one week}} \quad = \quad \frac{0.5\text{kg garbage/day}}{\text{average}}$$

You will eventually want about one pound of worms per cubic foot of volume in your bin. Since they will reproduce, you can start with about half that quantity. For the quantity of garbage shown above, I would start with two to three pounds of worms in a six cubic foot worm bin (1kg to 1.5kg in a 60 x 90 x 30cm worm bin).

Calculations for a household that produces a smaller amount of garbage are similar:

English *Units*	$\dfrac{3.5 \text{ lb garbage/week}}{7 \text{ days in one week}}$	=	1/2 lb garbage/day average
Metric *Units*	$\dfrac{1.6\text{kg garbage/week}}{7 \text{ days in one week}}$	=	225g garbage/day average

Following the suggested worm:garbage ratio of 2:1, use one pound of worms for one-half pound of daily garbage (500g worms for 225g daily garbage). Referring back to Chapter 3, your container size should provide about four square feet surface area, or one square foot for each pound of garbage per week. I would set up a 2' x 2' Worm Bin with one pound of worms (60cm x 60cm with 500g worms).

Breeders or bedrun?

There are no hard and fast rules to tell you whether to start with breeders or bedrun. Breeders will lay cocoons more quickly and increase the number of individuals sooner, but they usually cost more from commercial growers because of the labor required to sort them. Also, some growers think breeders take longer to adjust to new culture conditions than do bedrun worms.

Many redworm growers sell what they refer to as bedrun, also known as pit-run or run-of-pit, worms. These are worms of all sizes and ages, from which bait-sized worms may or may not have been removed. Since there could be between 150,000 to 200,000 hatchlings in a pound (330,000-440,000/kg), the number of bedrun worms in a pound will vary tremendously; however, 2000 is a figure commonly used (4400/kg).

If you can order bedrun by weight, you will certainly get more worms than if you purchase breeders by weight. These young, small worms will grow rapidly and be able to reproduce soon. If they adjust to their new home faster than breeders would have, you will be ahead starting with bedrun, especially if they are cheaper.

Whichever you start with, breeders or bedrun, when they produce more worms than the garbage you are feeding them will support, many will get smaller, some will slow reproduction, and others will die. Eventually, no matter how many worms you start with, the population will stabilize at about the biomass that can be supported by the amount of food they receive.

Sources of redworms

You may be able to find garden centers or local growers to provide your initial stock. If you buy redworms from bait dealers, expect to pay about twice as much as you would if you buy directly from a grower.

Another way to obtain the redworms you need to set up your home vermicomposting system is to order them from one of the commercial earthworm growers who advertise in classified ads of gardening and fishing magazines.

Redworms are easily packaged and shipped through the postal mail or private package-delivery systems. Some growers advertise and ship all year-round, others seasonally. As with growing conditions, temperature extremes should be avoided, but if the temperature is colder than 20°F (-6°C) or above 90°F (32°C), growers will usually wait until these temperatures moderate before they ship the worms.

Those of you who like adventure may be able to collect redworms from a compost pile or from their natural habitat. Your chances increase if you have a friend with horses, a barn, and a manure pile. You may have to turn over a lot of manure to find any, but then again, you could get lucky and find hundreds of worms in a few pitchforks full of moist manure at just the right stage of decomposition to support them.

8.
How do I set up my worm bin?

When you have completed tasks one through six on the checklist that appears on the flyleaf of this book, you are ready to set up your worm bin. You have determined approximately how many pounds of kitchen waste you dispose of per week, purchased or built your container accordingly, selected and obtained your bedding, and ordered or collected your worms. If all materials are on hand, it takes about an hour to set up your bin.

Preparation of worm bedding
Needed:
- Completed worm bin
- Bedding materials (see Chapter 4)
- 1 to 2 handfuls of soil
- Bathroom or utility scale
- Jug
- Large clean plastic or metal garbage can for mixing bedding

Paper bedding
The amount of bedding you need depends, or course, on the volume of your container. This can be a very rough measure. It is important to prepare enough bedding initially so that your container will be about three-quarters full with the moistened bedding in place. The comparable English and metric charts which follow provide the approximate weight of newspaper to set up several of the bins described in this book.

Type of bin	Cubic feet	Gallons	Pounds of bedding
2x2x8 box	2.7	19	8.0
1x2x3 box	5.8	43	17.5
Patio Bench	7.5	56	22.5
Worm-a-way Small	1.6	12	5.0
Worm-a-way Large	2.5	18	7.5

Figure 18. Capacities for bins and bedding are expressed in English units of cubic feet, gallons, and pounds.

A rule of thumb is to use about three pounds of newspaper per cubic foot volume of the bin (50g newspaper/liter). For plastic containers which give capacity in gallons, use about four-tenths pounds of paper per gallon. If you don't have a household utility scale, stand on a bathroom scale, first alone and then with your plastic bag full of dry

Type of bin	Volume liters	Bedding kilograms
60 x 60 x 20cm	70	3.6
30 x 60 x 90cm	152	8.0
30 x 60 x 100cm	177	10.0
Worm-a-way Small	69	3.4
Worm-a-way Large	42	2.3

Figure 19. Capacities for bins and bedding are expressed in metric units of cubic centimeters, liters, and kilograms.

bedding. The difference between the two weights, of course, is the weight of the bedding.

The major task remaining to set up your worm bin is to prepare the bedding for the worms by adding the proper amount of moisture; bedding should be damp, but not soggy. A worm's body consists of approximately 75 to 90% water, and its surface must be moist in order for the worm to "breathe." By preparing bedding with approximately the same moisture content (75%) as the worm's body, the worm doesn't have to combat an environment that is either too dry or too moist.

When using shredded paper bedding, a 75% moisture content can be easily obtained since the residual moisture present is minimal. Just weigh the bedding and add water equal to three times its weight. To get 75% moisture, for example, add fifteen pounds of water to five pounds of shredded newspaper bedding (6kg water to 2kg bedding). Or, expressed another way:

water:bedding ratio = 3:1 by weight

Because plastic bins tend to accumulate water, I usually recommend that you use about one-third less water

MIX BEDDING AND WATER

when setting up a plastic bin. I will discuss this more in Chapter 10.

Place about one-half of the bedding into the large mixing container. Add about one-half of the required amount of water and mix it into the bedding. Then add one to two handfuls of soil and the remaining bedding and water. Mix again until the water is well distributed throughout the bedding. Now dump the entire contents of the container into your worm bin and distribute it evenly. (The bedding absorbs the water so that little, if any, leaks from the holes in the bottom of the bin.) Your bin is now ready for the worms!

Manure bedding

If you are using manure for bedding, it is more difficult to determine how much water to add to obtain the proper moisture content since you don't know how much moisture is already in the manure. Basically, you want the manure damp, but not soggy. If you squeeze a handful and produce three to four drops of water, it's probably all right; twenty drops or a stream of water is too wet.

With manure beddings, remember to add water at least two days before you add worms. Then, if the manure heats up as it begins to compost, the worms won't die from the heat.

Using worms packaged by growers for shipping

Most growers package worms for shipping in peat moss, although other materials are used. Experienced shippers pack worms in a fairly dry bedding for two good business reasons:
- Shipping costs are great.
- There is no point in paying to ship excess
  amounts of water.

It is more important, however, to provide a satisfactory environment for the worms. Although worms need bedding with some moisture in it, too much moisture can intensify the effects of temperature extremes during shipping. In mid-summer when the temperature is likely to be 80° to 90°F (27° to 32°C), a drier bedding acts as insulation, plus provides sufficient oxygen for the worms. Too much moisture fills air spaces and the additional heat stimulates natural microorganisms associated with the worms to use up all available oxygen before the worms can get it. If they die, neither you nor I would want to open the box for the smell!

The insulation effect of a drier bedding for packaging also pertains to cold weather shipments of worms. Although the worms will lose some of their moisture to the bedding, they are better off than if they were to freeze because it was too moist and too cold.

If you receive worms that seem dry, assume that the worms will quickly regain their lost body moisture when they are placed in a properly prepared bedding. This should be done within a day or two. Responsible growers try to do what's best for the worms, guarantee their shipments, and provide information so that the customer knows what to expect.

If you need to hold your worms more than two days, open the box, sprinkle water on top to make the worms more comfortable, and add a light layer (a tablespoon or so per thousand worms) of oatbran on top. Feed again only when most of the food disappears in one or two days. Don't stir the grain into the bedding, or the bedding may become sour and/or overheat.

Adding the worms and garbage

When your bedding is ready to receive the worms, open their container and dump the entire contents on top of your freshly prepared bedding. Gently spread any clumps of worms around the surface. Leave the room lights on for awhile. The worms will gradually move down into the bedding as they try to avoid the light. Within a few minutes, the majority of worms will have disappeared into the bedding. If any remain on the surface after an hour, assume that they are either dead or unhealthy. Remove them.

Once the worms are down, you may start burying garbage. Of course you know the average amount of garbage your household produces in a week. Dig a hole big enough to accept the amount of garbage you are burying and dump the food waste into the hole. Draw enough bedding over the garbage to cover it completely.

An alternative method is to wrap peelings and other food waste in newspaper to keep them "contained," and add them as a package. This keeps them tidy, covered, and provides additional bedding. This method does require a bit more water.

With lidded containers, merely close the lid after the worms go down. The simpler boxes without lids require a piece of carpet, burlap, or sheet of black plastic to keep out the light and retain moisture. The worms work up to the surface; when you lift the plastic, you will see them scramble down into the bedding.

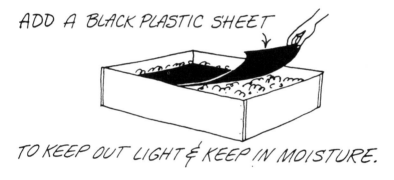

You've done it! Your worm bin is all set up. Now let's take a close look at your garbage. What does it really contain?

9.

What kind of garbage, and what do I do with it?

What's garbage to me may be trash to you, but slop for the pigs or food for the dog to someone else. I have previously used such terms as organic kitchen waste and table scraps. It's time to be more specific about what waste you can expect to feed to your worms.

FOOD WASTE

Vegetable waste

Any vegetable waste that you generate during food preparation can be used, such as potato peels, grapefruit and orange rinds, outer leaves of lettuce and cabbage, celery ends, and so forth. Plate scrapings might include macaroni, spaghetti, gravy, vegetables, or potatoes. Spoiled food from the refrigerator, such as baked beans, moldy cottage cheese, and leftover casserole also can go into the worm bin. Coffee grounds are very good in a worm bin, enhancing the texture of the final vermicompost. Tea leaves, even tea bags and coffee filters, are suitable.

Egg shells can go in as they are. I have found as many as 50 worms curled up in one egg shell. Usually, I dry them separately, then pulverize them with a rolling pin so they don't look quite so obvious when I finally put vermicom-

VARIETY OF FOOD WASTE FED TO WORMS

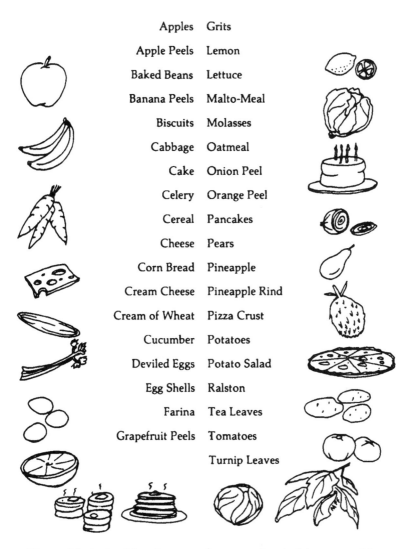

Apples	Grits
Apple Peels	Lemon
Baked Beans	Lettuce
Banana Peels	Malto-Meal
Biscuits	Molasses
Cabbage	Oatmeal
Cake	Onion Peel
Celery	Orange Peel
Cereal	Pancakes
Cheese	Pears
Corn Bread	Pineapple
Cream Cheese	Pineapple Rind
Cream of Wheat	Pizza Crust
Cucumber	Potatoes
Deviled Eggs	Potato Salad
Egg Shells	Ralston
Farina	Tea Leaves
Grapefruit Peels	Tomatoes
	Turnip Leaves

Figure 20. Actual food waste that was buried in worm bins during a demonstration project at the Kalamazoo Nature Center. Worms can also consume many wastes that do not appear on this list.

post in my garden. Grinding up egg shells also increases their surface area. This makes calcium carbonate more readily available to the microorganisms and other decomposers in the bin and, later, to plants in the garden.

Figure 20 shows some of the variety of food waste that can be fed to worms. It was developed from waste actually buried in worm bins at a Michigan nature center during a publicly-funded project in the 1970's. Coffee grounds don't appear on the list merely because none of the six participants' families drank coffee. Use this list as a guideline only; it is not, by any means, comprehensive.

Toxic components

Users have reported to me that excess quantities of citrus will kill worms. If you have a small bin and squeeze a dozen or so oranges for brunch guests, I advise you not to put all of the rinds in the bin. A teacher at a science convention reported to me that one of her ninth-grade students isolated the toxic material in citrus that killed the worms. She identified the substance as limonene, toxic to worms in very small concentrations.

I was, of course, skeptical that a ninth-grader could isolate and identify a specific chemical. Probing further, I learned that the teacher lived near a Dupont Chemical Company research facility. Since I live in Kalamazoo, home of a major pharmaceutical company with a commitment to science education, I realized that a student could have a well-placed parent with access to sophisticated labs, equipment, and knowledge. More power to the younger generation!

Meat waste and bones

You will not find any meat on the list of food waste in Figure 20. When designing the National Center for Appropriate Technology project at the nature center, we deliberately excluded the burial of meat to achieve these intents:

- **Avoid foul odors.**

    Decaying meat can produce offensive odors from the breakdown of proteins in a process known as putrefaction.

- **Reduce attraction to nuisance organisms.**
  Flies, mice, ants, and rats are likely to be attracted to a worm bin containing meat.
- **Prevent possible injury from sharp bones.**
  Although bones will eventually be "picked clean" by the worms, their sharp edges can injure your hands when you bury the garbage.
- **Enhance appearance of vermicompost.**
  Bones look unattractive when vermicompost containing them is used in gardens.

Since the demonstration bins were to be located in a public exhibit area and seen by thousands of visitors, it was important to avoid such potential problems.

Governments are giving increased attention to keeping organic wastes out of landfills. Some municipal and other governmental units sponsor worm bin distribution and educational programs to help achieve their goals. Almost all of them warn citizens to avoid putting meat, bones, and dairy products in household worm bins for the reasons given above.

In over two decades of having a worm bin in my home, I have found that the worms and associated microorganisms can handle some meat in a worm bin. I do bury chicken

bones, for example. If I dig too soon into the pocket of bedding containing the bones and decaying meat, the odor is bad. If I don't disturb it, I don't notice it. When I harvest the castings after several months, what remains is crumbly vermicompost which smells like damp, rich earth that contains darkened, well-picked bones.

One worm grower buried the bones from a community chicken barbeque in large outdoor worm bins. He said that it took only three weeks for the bones to be picked clean. Dr. Dan Dindal, State University of New York at Syracuse, suggests adding a good carbon source (such as sawdust or extra bedding) to meat and bones to speed-up decomposition time. He finds that if meat is chopped, ground, and thoroughly mixed with the carbon source, rodents won't even be a problem. He says, "I do this successfully all the time in outdoor piles." Several large-scale projects in India use vermicomposting to transform chicken processing waste into valuable natural fertilizer.

The previous examples indicate that some meat and bones can be successfully composted if sufficient cover is provided. Advantages exist for putting some of these nitrogen-rich materials into your worm bin. Worms require nitrogen in a form they can use. Nitrogen is also required by the microorganisms that do much of the composting and which are, in turn, eaten by the worms. Since meat contains protein, built from nitrogenous components, eliminating all meat from the system could result in a nutrient deficiency for the teeming organisms that constitute a home vermicomposting system. A further advantage of adding some meat is that more plant nutrients will be in vermicompost produced by worms which have consumed a greater variety of materials. Finally, putting meat scraps into your bin means you don't have to figure out another way to dispose of them.

Conversely, a disadvantage of not putting spoiled meat, meat scraps, and bones into your worm bin is that another way must be found to dispose of them. I do this by burying them in my garden. My personal feeling about burying bones and meat waste in a worm bin is that small amounts are all right. When I clean out my worm bin every six months to a year, I gather the bones into a net bag and hang them in the garage. The next time I clean out the bin and gather more bones, I process the old ones—now completely dry and brittle—by pounding them on concrete with a sledge hammer. These pulverized bones are added to my garden where plants benefit from their nutrients without my having to purchase bone meal for nitrogen, potassium, and phosphorus. And, centuries from now, the archeologists excavating my homesite won't have a clue that I was a meat-eater!

For the small system inside my home, I use judgment on the quantities of meat and bones that I bury. I put more of my meat, bones, and dairy wastes into my Patio Bench Worm Bin, away from my immediate living quarters. My advice to you is either avoid placing meat, bones, and dairy products in your worm bin or experiment cautiously with these high-nitrogen materials. Learn for yourself what your system can take within the design and demands you place upon it.

NO-NO'S

Non-biodegradables

Since what is obvious to some of us isn't always obvious to everyone else, let me suggest some things that don't belong in a worm bin: plastic bags, bottle caps, rubber bands, sponges, aluminum foil, and glass. Such non-biodegradable materials will stay there seemingly forever. They will clutter up your developing vermicompost and make it look more like trash. I have seen the same red rubber band over a three-year period in a large outdoor pit!

Pet feces

Dog feces also do not belong in the worm bin. Less obvious, but definitely to be guarded against, is letting a cat use your worm bin as a litter box. First of all, cat urine would soon make odor intolerable. Secondly, the ammonia in the urine could kill your worms. But the greatest concern has to do with a disease organism, called *Toxoplasma gondii*, that can be carried in the feces of cats. Tiny cysts of this protozoan can be inhaled by people and hidden in human tissues. Frequently no outward symptoms occur in the infected person, but it is possible that a pregnant woman could transmit toxoplasmosis to her fetus. A child born with brain damage could have been innocently harmed because *Toxoplasma gondii* was passed from the cat. Although most cats do not harbor this organism, any cat owner should be very careful in disposing of cat litter. If you have cats, keep them from using your worm bin as a litter box.

WASTE-HANDLING PROCEDURES

Collection

I hang a container above the sink to collect all of the organic waste that I will eventually feed to the worms. (Hanging it keeps our cats away from it.) I don't use a lid. This permits air to get to its contents and avoids the odors that will soon develop in a tightly closed container (see aerobic/anaerobic discussion, page 13). I have found that adding fresh waste to a tightly closed container becomes objectionable to me. These tightly closed containers can get pretty "ripe." I am also concerned that if I were to add the contents of the closed container to my worm bin, I would be introducing a large quantity of anaerobic bacteria to the system. Consequently, it would be more difficult to maintain the aerobic conditions we strive for in a worm composting system.

Frequency

About twice a week, I empty the contents of the holding container into my worm bin. If I have a lot of waste to get rid of, I empty it more often; if I don't have much, less often. In other words, I don't concern myself with seeing to it that the worms are fed daily, twice a week, or even weekly. My needs, not the worms', dictate how often the worms get fed.

Location

Because I keep records of how much garbage I bury in my worm bins, I weigh the garbage. As I record the weight, I also check my record sheet to see where I buried garbage the last time. I rotate around the box, placing garbage in different areas in sequence like this:

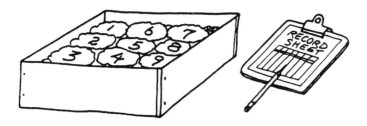

Figure 21. Burial spots are recorded.

How do you feed your worms? Or, how do you place your food waste in the bin? The bin I use has about nine locations where I can bury the garbage before I have to re-use a spot. Since I bury garbage about twice a week, four and a half weeks pass before I have to dig into a region already containing garbage. By then, much of it is no longer recognizable, having been consumed by the worms or having been broken down by the other natural decomposition processes caused by worm associates in the box.

Post-burial actions

I cover the newly deposited waste with an inch or two (2.5-5cm) of bedding, adding more bedding frequently. Covering it makes the food waste less accessible for flies to lay their eggs, and adding bedding adds more of a carbon source for the worms. (The alternative method of wrapping food waste in newspaper means it's already covered with bedding.) Then I close the lid or replace the sheet of plastic I have lying loosely on top to retain moisture. With that, I'm through! The whole process takes maybe two minutes, *if* I take the time to poke around looking for cocoons or baby worms.

The worms will tend to follow the waste, but not necessarily when it is fresh. Garbage will undergo many changes as different kinds of microorganisms invade tissues, breaking them down and creating an environment for other kinds of organisms to feed and reproduce. The worms undoubtedly consume some of the cells from which these tissues are made, but the worms feed also on the bacteria, protozoa, and fungi that thrive in this moist, warm, food-rich environment. Although this book is titled *Worms Eat My Garbage*, I must acknowledge that worms, springtails, sowbugs, bacteria, protozoa, and fungi eat my garbage. The worms are there because they help keep conditions aerobic and therefore odor-free, reduce the mass of material to be processed, and produce castings far richer than mere compost. Worms don't do the job alone.

Handling techniques

Techniques vary for handling food waste. One vegetarian who uses worms to process her kitchen waste has large quantities of peelings, wheat grass roots, and pulp from juicing carrots, celery, and other vegetables. Her container is a galvanized garbage can with aeration holes drilled in the lid and top half of the sides. She adds waste daily, merely lifting the lid and dropping the waste onto the surface of the bedding. Occasionally, she throws a double-handful of peat on top of the mass when the lid is lifted. Masses of worms can be seen feeding on  the recently deposited waste. Odor has not been a problem in this system. The worms have reproduced greatly, and the end product appears to be well-converted vermicompost.

Should you grind the garbage? No, not for most home systems. Eventually, any soft food waste will break down to become vermicompost, even citrus and melon rinds. I have mentioned that I do pulverize egg shells with a rolling pin to reduce the size of their pieces. There is no question that worms can eat ground food waste more readily than large particles of food. A worm's mouth is tiny, and it has no teeth to break down food particles. Sometimes the finely ground materials will become anaerobic and putrefy, and distress your worms.

Part of my rationale for using worms inside the home to process food waste is to reduce dependence upon technology. The energy required to grind garbage, dilute it with water, and flush it down the drain, as well as for processing it at the wastewater treatment plant can be better used elsewhere. For me, to regularly grind garbage before feeding it to worms is inconsistent with why I use worms in the first place.

Overloading the system

A common and appropriate question is, "Can I put too much garbage in the worm bin?" Yes. You may have a greater than normal quantity of food waste during holidays or harvest activities such as canning or bottling. If you deposit all of it in your worm bin, you may find that you have overloaded the system. When this happens, it is more likely that anaerobic conditions will develop, causing odor. The first thing I would do to eliminate odor is aerate the bin by turning the material; this will disturb your worms. I would also add fresh bedding. If you can leave it long enough without adding any fresh waste, the problem will usually correct itself. This does present you with the problem of how to dispose of your normal quantity of food waste during the interim.

A possible approach to the "overload" times is to set up a separate container with fresh bedding and use a half-bucket of vermicompost from your original bin to inoculate this new container with worms and microorganisms. This bin could be maintained minimally, feeding the worms only on the occasions when your week's garbage far exceeds the amount for which your main bin was constructed.

I have used an old leaky galvanized washtub as a "worm bin annex," that I kept outside near the garage. During canning season the grape pulp, corn cobs, corn husks, bean cuttings, and other fall harvest residues went into this container. It got soggy when it rained, and the worms grew huge from all the food and moisture. We brought it inside at about the time of the first frost. The worms kept working the material until there was no food left. After six to eight months, the only identifiable remains were a few corn cobs, squash seeds, tomato skins, and some nondecomposed corn husks. The rest was an excellent batch of worm castings and a very few hardy, undernourished worms.

In other words, given enough time, practically any amount of organic material will eventually break down and decompose in a worm culture. When you want to add fresh material every week, as you do in a system being used to dispose of kitchen waste, there are limits to what is reasonable to add at one time. Your nose is probably the best guide as to when that limit has been exceeded.

10.
How do I take care
of my worms?

One favorable aspect of having "worms as pets" is that you can go away without having to make boarding arrangements with the vet or a neighbor. You can go away for a weekend, a week, even two weeks, and not worry about your worms. However, if you plan to go for a month or more, or plan to turn off the heat while away on a winter vacation, you should probably board them out while you are gone.

Tender loving care for worms basically means respecting them as living organisms. Worm workers provide them with the proper environment and nutrition, check them occasionally, and leave them alone. The less you disturb them, the better off the worms will be, even though you make some observations of what goes on in their box. Once your worm bin is set up with bedding of the proper moisture content, several sheets of damp newspaper or a sheet of plastic lying loosely on top will retain that moisture. Daily care is unnecessary.

Learning

Burial of garbage, whether it is done weekly or more often, consists merely of pushing bedding aside to create a large enough pocket to contain the garbage, depositing the garbage, and covering it with an inch or so of bedding. Train yourself to make a few observations at these times. Does the bedding seem to be drying around the edges? Where are the worms congregating? To find out, you will have to push bedding aside in areas where you have deposited garbage. You can use your hands to do this, or you may prefer to use a trowel or a small hand tool similar to what I call my "worm fork." A worm fork is less likely to injure worms than a trowel.

Sometimes you will see masses of worms feeding around something that especially appeals to them. For curiosity's sake, you might want to note their preference. My worms, for example, love watermelon rind. I place the rind, flesh side down, on the surface of the bedding. Within the next two days, masses of worms of all ages congregate underneath the rind. Within three weeks, all that remains is the very outer part of the rind, looking a lot like a sheet of paper. The same is true for cantaloupe, pumpkin, and squash. Some worm workers have seen worms devouring fresh onion. Odor, if any, won't last long.

There are many other things you can observe. Do older worms prefer different food than younger worms? When do you first find cocoons? Are they deposited on top of or throughout the bedding? Are any worms mating? Do you see differences in the degree to which the clitellum is swollen?

The preceding questions barely suggest the rich learning experience a home vermicomposting system can provide. Children are fascinated by worms. Many will find the system is an ideal science project. Even a three-year-old was able to understand the concept of feeding garbage to worms. She asked her mother, "Mommy, do I throw this in the garbage can or do I feed it to the worms?"

Record-keeping
I mentioned previously that I keep records of my worm bin activities. In fact, my records from the past 25 years provided much of the information in this book. Some of you

will want to keep records also, although this would be a distasteful chore for others. If you decide to keep records, it will help to have a utility scale for weighing the garbage and a thermometer for determining bedding temperature. I currently use a data sheet similar to similar to the one in Appendix A.

Solving excess water problems

Plastic worm bins in damp locations, such as basements, tend to accumulate excess moisture in the bottom of the bin. This water comes from several sources. You added water to the bedding when you first set up your bin. Secondly, you add more water every time you add food waste because 80-90% of food waste is water. The third source, however, comes from the water produced by the microorganisms and worms as they break down the waste, giving off carbon dixide and water as end products. The water vapor produced during these metabolic processes condenses on the smooth, non-porous walls of the plastic container. This condensation water picks up dissolved nutrients as it trickles down through the vermicompost to the bottom. It is sometimes referred to as "castings tea" or "vermicompost tea," but clearly not for human consumption. Following are several ways to solve the problem of excess moisture, especially in plastic bins.

Drain and catch

The bottoms of some plastic bins have drainage holes or an open mesh. A tray underneath holds the water that drains through. This seems reasonable because no one wants drainage water flowing onto the basement floor. It has a potentially unfavorable consequence, however, pointed out by the environmental toxicologist Dr. Michael Bisesi.

When Dr. Bisesi compared the effectiveness of two types of plastic worm bins, he expressed reservations about the system design which relied upon a catchment tray to hold the dark water that drained through the vermicompost. His concern was that the nutrient-rich broth could provide ideal culture conditions for many organisms not subject to the controls inside the worm bin. Unchecked, these cultures could proliferate numbers of bacteria and molds in the open where "Yuck" would be a typical response. Open trays like this would not be considered acceptable in most classrooms.

Add dry bedding

I have found that adding dry shredded paper to the surface of the worm bin every two to three weeks helps to reduce excess moisture problems. As the vapor pressure inside the bin increases, the water vapor condenses on the lid and "rains" on the new dry bedding, making it damp. Within a few days, the excess moisture distributes itself throughout the bin, and water standing in the bottom is less of a problem. The worms seem to like the oxygen-rich layer near the fresh bedding on the surface. I frequently find many of them present in the vermicompost at the surface just underneath the bedding. Regular additions of the carbon-source which bedding provides also seem to improve functioning of the whole system.

Draw off with a turkey baster

Much of the liquid at the bottom is waste excreted by the worms and not good in their living space. Some people

collect this excess liquid so they can apply diluted quantities of it to their house plants. A turkey baster comes in handy to perform this task. I have found that it's easier to use the turkey baster when I press a strainer into the soggy bedding in the bottom of the bin. Vermicompost tea seeps through and is easily drawn up into the turkey baster without having bedding clog the opening.

Pour off or drain
Tilting the bin and holding the bedding back while you pour off the vermicompost tea is possible, but may require two people to do the job. If the previous techniques don't work, and your bin is in a location where excess water is a continual problem, I would recommend drilling one hole near the bottom of one side of the bin and plugging it with a cork or rubber stopper. On the few occasions when you have to drain it, just remove the plug. Of course, bins with spigots in the bottom have already made draining off vermicompost tea easy to do, although you may have to poke something inside the spigot occasionally to maintain the opening if it gets clogged.

Make a peat-moss "worm"
A Kalamazoo worm worker, Jean DeMott, shared with me her ingenious way of dealing with excess water in her basement worm bin. She reused an old pair of panty-hose by cutting one leg off and filling it with peat moss. Closing both ends with rubber bands, she placed the giant peat-moss "worm" deep into her worm bin and let it absorb the vermicompost tea. She then used the peat moss which contained all the nutrients from the worm bin as part of her potting mixture when she repotted plants.

MAINTENANCE PROCEDURES

Changing the bedding
In about six weeks you may begin to see noticeable changes in the bedding. It will get darker, and you will be able to identify individual castings. Although you add food waste regularly, the bedding volume will slowly decrease.

As more of the bedding and garbage is converted to earthworm castings, extensive decomposition and composting by other organisms in the bin also take place. I mentioned earlier that the proportion of castings increases as the environmental quality for your worms decreases. There will come a time when so much of the bedding in the box becomes castings that the worm population will suffer. Because each system is different— depending upon bedding used, quantity of worms, types of garbage fed to them, bin temperature, and moisture conditions—it is not possible to predict precisely when you must deal with changing the environment of your worms. It is important to get them away from their castings and to prepare fresh bedding for them at the right time.

Your particular goals, described in Chapter 2 in terms of whether they require high, low, or medium levels of maintenance, will help decide this. That is, to harvest extra worms for fishing, you will have to change bedding more frequently. Plan on doing this every two to three months, and figure that it is a high-maintenance system.

Harvesting worms

If you don't want to harvest worms from partially decomposed garbage and bedding, but do want high-quality vermicompost almost fully converted to worm castings, the trade-off is losing your worm population. Accepting this trade-off means adapting your own behaviors to complement this loss. In northern systems, for example, you might bury garbage in your bin for the four winter months, and then let it sit unattended for another three to four months. By July you will find a bin full of fine, black worm castings, but there will be very few worms remaining—perhaps not more than a dozen. These fine castings can be used as top dressing on your house plants and in your garden for a late shot of nutrients. This was referred to earlier as the "lazy person's" technique for maintaining a worm bin. I've done it, and it does work. When I'm using this system though, I have to compost food waste in outdoor compost piles during spring, summer, and fall.

High- and medium-maintenance systems require that you harvest the worms, or at least give them the opportunity to move into fresh bedding. For a high-maintenance system, plan to do this every two to three months, while medium-maintenance means going about four months before you take action. Your first-time harvest of a 2x2 bin takes two to three hours, but it goes faster when you gain some experience. If you have curious friends or family to help, even faster harvests are possible.

The illustrator of this book finds it therapeutic to sort worms. Her illustrations come from years of first-hand experience of separating worms from their castings.

Dump and hand sort
Needed:
- Very large sheet of heavy plastic
- Goose-neck or similar lamp with 100-watt bulb, if you work inside
- Plastic dish pan or other container for worms
- Plastic or metal garbage can, corrugated carton, or heavy-duty plastic bag for vermicompost
- Fresh bedding

Spread the plastic sheet on the ground, floor, or table, and dump the entire contents of the worm bin on the plastic. Make about nine pyramid-shaped piles. You should see worms all over the place. If the light is bright enough, they quickly move away from it and head toward the center of each vermicompost pile. Impatient worm workers start hand-picking worms from this point on, gently scraping compost from the top of each pile, putting worms into the worm container as they find them.

You may prefer to leave the piles alone five to ten minutes. When you return you won't see any worms. Gently remove the outer surface of each pile. As you do so, worms on the newly exposed surface will again react to the light

HARVESTING TECHNIQUE:
DUMP AND HAND SORT.

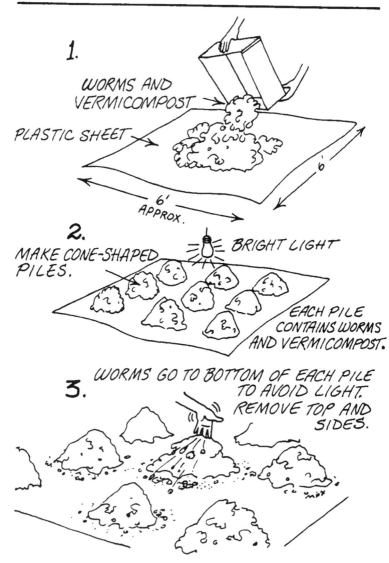

1.

WORMS AND VERMICOMPOST

PLASTIC SHEET

6'

6' APPROX.

2. MAKE CONE-SHAPED PILES.

BRIGHT LIGHT

EACH PILE CONTAINS WORMS AND VERMICOMPOST.

3. WORMS GO TO BOTTOM OF EACH PILE TO AVOID LIGHT. REMOVE TOP AND SIDES.

Figure 22. Dump and hand sort is an effective way to separate worms from their castings.

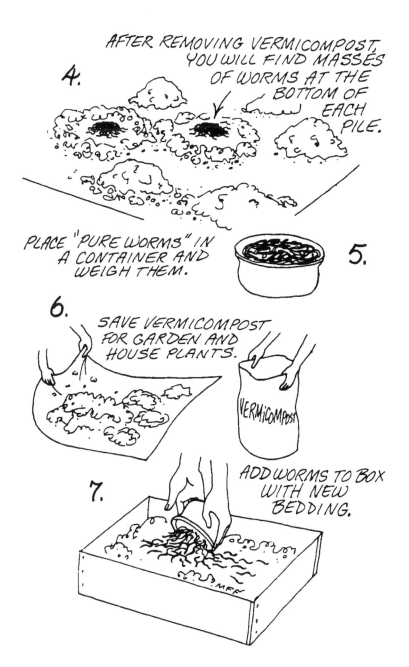

4. AFTER REMOVING VERMICOMPOST, YOU WILL FIND MASSES OF WORMS AT THE BOTTOM OF EACH PILE.

PLACE "PURE WORMS" IN A CONTAINER AND WEIGH THEM. **5.**

6. SAVE VERMICOMPOST FOR GARDEN AND HOUSE PLANTS.

VERMICOMPOST

7. ADD WORMS TO BOX WITH NEW BEDDING.

Figure 22, continued.

and retreat toward the interior. By following this procedure one pile at a time, you will find that when you return to the first pile, the worms will have disappeared again, and you can repeat the procedure.

Eventually, the worms will aggregate in a mass at the bottom of each pile. Remove the vermicompost that collects on top of them, and put the worms in the container you have ready for them. You will be amazed at the mass of "pure worms" you get from this technique. Only if you are going to weigh the worms do you need to remove all vermicompost from this batch. During this process, you or someone else should be making up fresh bedding and restocking the worm bin. When the bedding is ready and the worms are sorted and weighed, add them to the top of the bin as you did originally. You are now ready for another cycle.

- Vermicompost from this sorting process will vary in consistency, depending upon how long the bin has been going, how much and what kind of garbage was buried, and how much decomposition has occurred. Some of the most recently buried food waste can be put right back into the fresh bedding. The rest can continue to vermicompost in the plastic bag or garbage can you assembled earlier for conducting the harvest.
- Vermicompost from plastic bins may be excessively moist. If water drains onto the plastic sheet, or if the pile slumps down from the excess water, you know it is too wet. Sorting through this sticky material is not pleasant, and it is very difficult to get the worms out.

I have placed such soggy vermicompost in a heavy-duty corrugated container and let it sit in a dry place for several weeks. So much excess moisture evaporated from the surface and through the walls of the box during those weeks, the compost lost 15 pounds (7kg), or about one-third of its original weight. After losing this much water, the vermicompost was well-stabilized and earthy-smelling. It had a crumbly texture perfect for use in my garden. The worms I found were tiny, however, and could obviously have benefited from some new food and drink.

A large number of cocoons and baby worms should be present in the vermicompost from which worms were harvested. If you wish, you can save many of them by letting the vermicompost sit for about three weeks. Then attract them with a long, narrow strip of food. This may be one occasion where use of a blender is appropriate.

Make a slurry of garbage, perhaps with some oatmeal, cornmeal, or other grain mash in it. With your fingers or a trowel, make a groove down the center of the vermicompost, and fill this groove with the slurry. In a couple of days, you should be able to remove concentrated batches of young worms from underneath this narrow strip. Repeat two or three times to obtain new hatchlings as they come along. You can add these new worms to your regular bin.

Let the worms do the sorting

If you don't want to deal with the "Dump and Hand Sort" method described above, ways to avoid that process exist, especially if you aren't interested in knowing the weight of your worms.

When the bedding has diminished to the extent that it is not deep enough to make a hole to bury fresh garbage, it is time to add fresh bedding. Prepare about one-half the original quantity of fresh bedding. Pull all of the vermicompost in your bin over to one side, and add the new bedding to the empty side. Bury your garbage in the new bedding, and let the worms find their way to it. It is helpful to replace the plastic sheet only on the side with the fresh bedding to permit the other side to dry out more rapidly.

Every two to three months, you can remove the vermicompost, replace it with more fresh bedding, and keep going back and forth from one side to the other in this manner. The vermicompost you remove will still have some worms in it, but enough should have migrated to the new bedding so that you needn't worry about harvesting the few that remain.

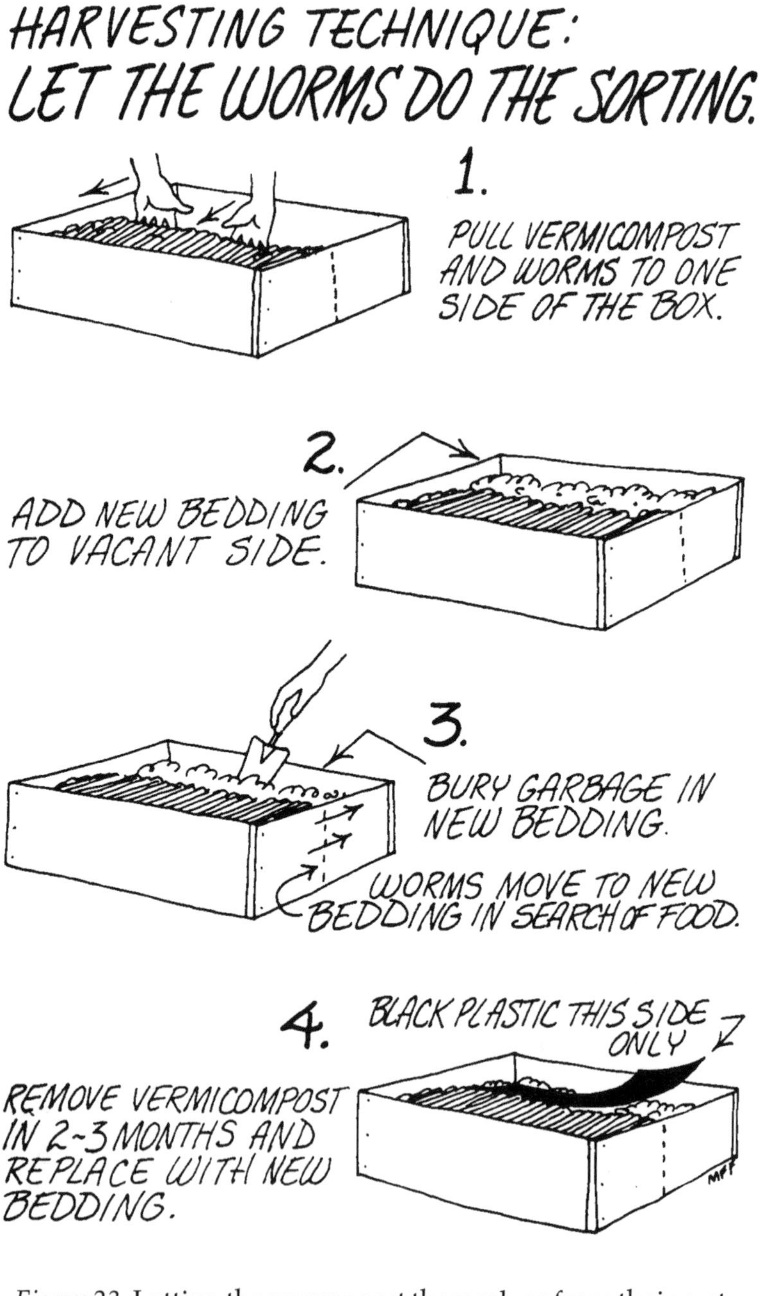

HARVESTING TECHNIQUE:
LET THE WORMS DO THE SORTING.

1.

PULL VERMICOMPOST AND WORMS TO ONE SIDE OF THE BOX.

2.

ADD NEW BEDDING TO VACANT SIDE.

3.

BURY GARBAGE IN NEW BEDDING.

WORMS MOVE TO NEW BEDDING IN SEARCH OF FOOD.

4. BLACK PLASTIC THIS SIDE ONLY

REMOVE VERMICOMPOST IN 2~3 MONTHS AND REPLACE WITH NEW BEDDING.

Figure 23. Letting the worms sort themselves from their castings saves worm workers' time.

Some commercial bins use an effective variation of this self-sort technique by placing a vertical mesh or perforated screen between the two halves of the worm bin. Worm workers place food waste in one side for a period of time, then use the other side. The worms freely move horizontally through the mesh or screen holes on their own time. Eventually the side with the fresher material has more worms, and the older side has stabilized vermicompost which can be removed.

The Can-O-Worms™ described in Chapter 3 improves upon the horizontal method of letting the worms do the sorting by having the worms move up toward the new supply of food, leaving their castings in the lower trays. Our experience with this vertical system is that the lower trays become full of finely processed castings with no recognizable food waste. The lower trays also have a lot of worms. It's easy to sort the worms from the well-processed castings by picking them out or dumping the tray. We have found that not all of the worms make it to the upper levels where the fresh food is.

Alternate containers

Many people find it most convenient to have more than one worm bin, one active and the other resting. When they can no longer find a suitable place in the first worm bin to bury food waste, they let it sit. They merely set up another bin with fresh bedding and soil, move some worms over from the first bin, and use the new bin exclusively. Meanwhile, the worms and microorganisms remaining in the first bin continue to process the waste which eventually stabilizes to consist of well-processed castings.

Divide and dump

Still another method for harvesting worms is the divide and dump technique. You simply remove about two-thirds of your vermicompost and dump it directly onto your garden's surface. No digging nor turning; no muss, no fuss. Add fresh bedding to the vermicompost still left in the box. Enough worms and cocoons usually remain there to populate the system for another cycle.

HARVESTING TECHNIQUE:
DIVIDE AND DUMP.

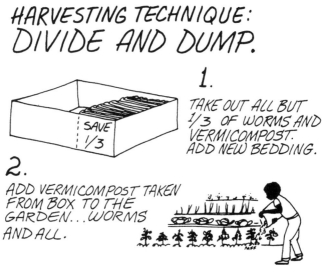

1.
TAKE OUT ALL BUT ⅓ OF WORMS AND VERMICOMPOST. ADD NEW BEDDING.

SAVE ⅓

2.
ADD VERMICOMPOST TAKEN FROM BOX TO THE GARDEN...WORMS AND ALL.

Figure 24. Divide and dump is a straightforward technique.

The maintenance system you choose will depend upon your preference, your lifestyle, and perhaps your schedule at the time. You may find yourself using all of these systems at various times. At any rate, maintaining your home vermicomposting system can be a flexible process and is really very simple.

TEMPERATURE EXTREMES

We've already discussed the need to maintain a worm-bin temperature that will permit the worms to thrive. What if I live where it gets too cold for the worms in the winter or too hot for them in the summer? Three approaches for each extreme are feasible. Let's consider cold winters first.

Winter methods
Bring the bin indoors
If it's warm enough inside your home for you, it's warm enough for the worms. Older people who prefer an indoor winter temperature of 80°F (27°C) or higher may find their worms prospering. Most people prefer to keep their worm bin in the basement. Apartment dwellers and those with no basements make room for their worm bin in their kitchen,

utility room, or even a living room! In a basement colder than 40°F (4°C), most worms will live, but move and eat very slowly. The worms and their associated composting organisms will not process as much food waste as if they were closer to their optimum temperature of 68° to 77°F (20° to 25°C). Use of a 7-watt night-light within the bin should bring the temperature up, although the light will inhibit their activity. The worms can work in the dark under a few sheets of newspaper.

Insulate your outdoor bin

To meet the demands of cold Canadian winters near Toronto, Sam Hambly, a worm grower, enthusiast, and educator, designed a worm bin two by four by four feet on a

side (60cm x 120cm x 120cm). The sides were plywood panels held together with screen door hooks and eyes, and the open bottom gave worms access to the soil beneath. (Or, the worms beneath had access to the goodies above!) Styrofoam®, a tradename of the Dow Chemical Company, provided insulation as four sheets of two-inch

Figure 25 (above). Sam Hambly points out features of his bottomless insulated worm bin suitable for Canadian winters.

Figure 26 (right). Corner detail shows fitted Styrofoam, hook, and eyes.

(5cm) pieces cut to fit inside the plywood walls.

Sam built a plywood lid with strips of wood along the edges that helped hold the unit together when in position. One of the most important design parts was a thick, supplemental Styrofoam lid. Sam cut the lid about four inches (10cm) smaller than the inside opening for placement directly on a plastic vapor barrier sitting on the bedding. The space around the sides allowed air to get to both the decomposing materials and the worms. He put leaves and garden residue in addition to food waste in this large bin. The large volume of organic materials inside this bin generated heat from its composting, and the "floating" lid retained enough of this heat to keep the worms warm and active even during the coldest parts of the winter.

Add supplemental heat

For years I have set up worm bins either in my garage or outdoors, trying to find the right combination of insulation and supplemental heat to keep my worms from freezing during our southern Michigan winters which can reach 15°F below zero (-10°C). I now place bales of straw around my Patio Bench Worm Bin and lay a one-inch (2.5cm) Styrofoam sheet inside the lid for insulation. I then insert a birdbath water heater with an electric immersion coil into a two-gallon (8-liter) jug of 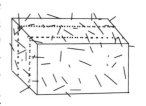 water. I wrap the connection between the heating coil and extension cord carefully with a plastic bag and electrical tape to prevent moisture from getting into the connection. This unit is plugged in throughout the winter. The thermostat turns the unit on when the temperature goes below 40°F (4°C), and maintains the water at that temperature. A fish-tank heater also works.

Even though the outside edges of the worm bin may freeze, I can always find some live worms near the central core containing the water. A thermostat set at 65°F (18°C) would produce more active worms, but would also consume more electricity. My main garbage disposal in the winter is my basement worm bin, so the outside "annex" doesn't receive very much food waste. In our household of two, we definitely do not produce enough food waste to keep a worm bin the size of Sam Hambly's going during the winter.

Summer methods
Bring the bin indoors
I have less experience with temperatures that are too hot for the worms, so I have to rely on information from those who live in warmer climates. Temperatures above 86°F (30°C) could start to cause problems. At 95°F (35°C) the worms are vulnerable to overheating and could die. At that temperature the worms have a much higher demand for oxygen, so they will deplete their bedding of oxygen much more quickly than at cooler temperatures. If some of the worms die, their bodies quickly begin to decompose, which removes even more oxygen. Some people find the easiest solution is to bring the worm bin indoors where it can be kept out of the sun.

Keep the bin in the shade
Often it is enough to place the worm bin under a tree where there is enough shade to keep direct sunlight from bearing down on the bin. Placement in a garage or under a shed roof also may work. If the exterior of your worm bin is a dark color, you may lessen absorption of heat by taping some aluminum foil (or re-use an aluminum-mylar potato chip bag) to the top of the bin to reflect heat away from the bin inself.

Use evaporative cooling
Some people drape a burlap bag around their worm bins, wet it, and lower the temperature inside by moving air across the wet cloth. A breeze is best, but use a fan if necessary. The process of evaporating water from the cloth removes heat from the bin in the same way that we cool down when we wear a wet shirt. Often, the period of critically high temperatures is relatively brief, so one doesn't have to take extraordinary measures like this for very long to keep your worms healthy.

11.
What are the most commonly asked questions about worms?

Are you one of the thousands of people who have mixed reactions towards worms? Do you feel revulsion towards these moist wriggly creatures at the same time that you are fascinated by them? Are you somewhat curious, but don't want to learn too much about them? Then this chapter is for you.

Can a worm see?

Contrary to the popular cartoon image of worms, they have no eyes and cannot see. They are, however, sensitive to light, particularly at their front ends. If a worm has been in the dark and is then exposed to bright light, it will quickly try to move away from the light. A nightcrawler, for example, will immediately retract into its burrow if you shine a flashlight on it some wet spring night.

The sensory cells in a worm's skin are less sensitive to red light than to light of mixed wavelengths. If you want to observe worms under less intrusive conditions, you can take advantage of this fact by placing red cellophane or an amber bread wrapper over your light source. You can make further observations of earthworm behavior in a photographic darkroom using a red safelight. Your eyes will adapt to the lower level of light these aids provide, and the worm will move more naturally than it does under bright light.

Where is the worm's mouth?

A worm's front and back ends are more technically known as anterior and posterior. The mouth is in the first anterior segment. A small, sensitive pad of flesh called the **prostomium** protrudes above the mouth. When the anterior end of the worm contracts, the prostomium is likely to plug the entrance to the mouth. When the worm is foraging for food, the prostomium stretches out, sensing suitable particles for the worm to ingest. I was amazed at how wide a nightcrawler can open its mouth when I first saw it on video. The worm curled its anterior segments upwards, revealing a wide-open mouth for a fraction of a second. Later, I saw the worm grab a leaf with its mouth and drag it towards its burrow.

Does a worm have teeth?

No. The mouth and pharynx are highly muscular, but they do not contain teeth.

How does a worm grind its food?

Because worms have no teeth, they have little capacity to grind their food. They are limited to food that is small enough to be drawn into the mouth. Usually this food is softened by moisture or by bacterial action. Bacteria, protozoa, and fungi undoubtedly help break down the ingested organic material. Every worm has one muscular **gizzard**, however, which functions similarly to gizzards in birds. Small grains of sand and mineral particles lodge in the giz-

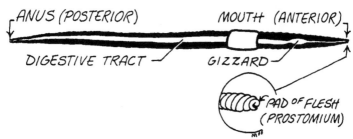

zard. Muscular contractions in the gizzard wall compress these hard materials against each other and the food, mix it with some fluid, and grind all into smaller particles. One reason for manually spreading a handful of topsoil, rock dust, or lime into worm bedding is to provide worms with small, hard particles for their gizzards.

What happens to food once it leaves the gizzard?

The ground-up food enters the worm's intestine, which secretes digestive enzymes to chemically break down molecules of food nutrients. These simplified nutrients then pass through the intestinal wall for absorption into the bloodstream, and are carried where needed. Undigested material, including soil, bacteria, and plant residues, passes out of the worm through its anus as a worm casting.

Do worms need air?

Worms require gaseous oxygen from the air. The oxygen diffuses across their moist skin tissue from the region of greater concentration of oxygen (the air) to that of lower concentration (inside the worm). When water has been sufficiently aerated, worms have been known to live under water for a considerable length of time.

Carbon dioxide produced by the bodily processes of the worm also diffuses through its moist skin. Also moving from higher concentration to lesser concentration, carbon dioxide moves from inside the worm's body out into the surrounding bedding. A constant supply of fresh air throughout the bedding helps this desirable exchange of gases take place.

If a worm is cut in half, will both parts grow back?

Worms do have a remarkable capacity to regenerate lost or injured parts, but this capacity is limited.

The cutting-a-worm-in-half myth.

Depending upon where the worm was cut, the anterior end can grow a new tail. The tail, however, cannot regenerate a new head. The capacity to regenerate new tissue is a form of reproduction among some animal forms, but not among earthworms. On rare occasions you may find a worm with two tails, both at the same end. This condition can be caused by injury to the worm in the posterior end, which results in growth of a new tail adjacent to the original tail.

Do worms die in the bin?

Worms undoubtedly die in any home worm bin, but if your box is properly maintained, you rarely will see a dead worm. Their bodies quickly decompose and are cleaned up by the other organisms in the box, leaving few dead worms you can recognize.

If large quantities of worms seem to be dying, you should attempt to determine the cause and correct the problem. Is it too hot? Are toxic gases building up in the bedding that cause the worms to surface and get away? Did you stress the worms by adding too much salty, aromatic, or acid-producing food?

You'll need to make some educated guesses about what the problem is, and try to correct it. Adding fresh bedding to a portion of the box sometimes is enough to correct the situation, by providing a safe environment towards which the worms can crawl.

How long does a worm live?

Most worms probably live and die within the same year. Especially in the field, most species are exposed to hazards such as dryness, weather that is too cold or too hot, lack of food, or predators. In culture, individuals of *Eisenia fetida* have been kept as long as four and a half years, and some *Lumbricus terrestris* have lived even longer.

If reading this far has served merely to whet your appetite for learning more about earthworms, the publications listed in Appendix B: "Annotated references" are books with more detailed information.

12.
What are some other critters in my worm bin?

Once your home vermicomposting system has been established for awhile, you will begin to find creatures other than earthworms present. This is a normal situation, but could be alarming if you were brought up to think that all bugs are bad bugs. Most of them are, in fact, good "bugs," and few of them actually are classified biologically as bugs. They play important roles in breaking down organic materials to simpler forms that can then be reassembled into other kinds of living tissue. This whole array of decomposer organisms gives meaning to the term, "recyclers." You could spend a lifetime studying the various creatures in a worm bin trying to determine who eats whom and under what conditions.

A scientist who has spent years studying the complex interrelationships among organisms found in compost piles and decaying litter is Dr. Dan Dindal. It was he who suggested that grinding meat and mixing it with a carbon source made meat scraps a useful component of garbage fed to worms (see page 66). Dr. Dindal developed the drawing in Figure 27 to illustrate what many of these organisms look like and how they relate to each other. Energy flows from organism to organism as one is eaten by the other in a natural recycling system. Snails, beetles, millipedes, centipedes, and ants are less likely to find their way to worm bins set up with shredded paper beddings.

Organisms that consume waste directly are first-level (1°) consumers. They include microscopic actinomycetes, molds, and bacteria. Actinomycetes are fungus-like bacteria that produce thin filaments radiating from a central point. Their presence gives compost and soil its "earthy" odor. Earthworms, beetle mites, sowbugs, enchytraeids, and flies are also first-level consumers when they consume waste directly.

Second-level (2°) consumers eat 1° consumers or their waste products. Examples of 2° consumers in a compost pile include springtails, mold mites, and feather-winged beetles that eat molds, bacteria, and actinomycetes. When protozoa and rotifers eat bacteria, they function as 2° consumers. The function an organism serves, however, changes depending upon its food source at a particular time. An organism may be a 1° consumer at one time, such as when an earthworm eats a leaf, or it may be a 2° consumer when it consumes the bacteria that cause a piece of apple to decay.

Third-level (3°) consumers are flesh-eaters, or predators, which eat 1° and 2° consumers. Predators in a compost pile or in your worm bin might include centipedes, rove beetles, ants, and predatory mites.

You won't be able to see many of the organisms pictured in Figure 27 because they are microscopic (bacteria, protozoa, nematodes, and rotifers). Others, such as the springtails and mites, are so small that you will probably need a hand lens to get a better look. Brief descriptions of the more common "critters" follow.

Enchytraeids

Known commonly as white worms or pot worms, enchytraeids are small (one-fourth to one inch, 10-25mm long), white, segmented worms. You might mistake them for newly hatched redworms because of their size. However, newly hatched redworms are reddish because of their red blood. Although related to the larger earthworms, enchytraeids do not have a hemoglobin-based blood, and remain white throughout their lifetime.

Enchytraeids eat decomposing plant material rich in microorganisms, but they digest only part of it, just like the

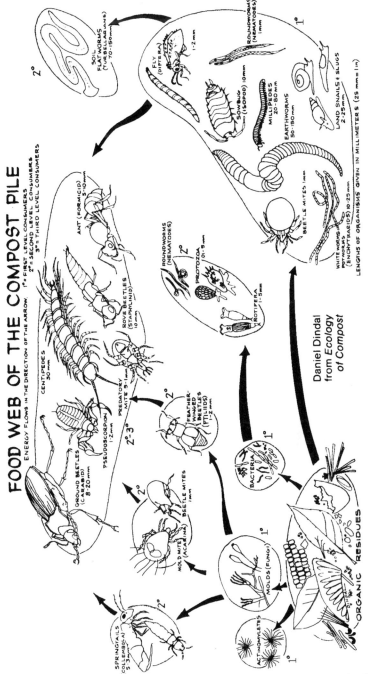

Figure 27. Organisms commonly found in compost include both plants and animals.

earthworms. This partial breakdown of litter helps make food material available for other decomposers. Their manure provides further sites for other microbial activity.

Some worm growers incorrectly call enchytraeids, "nematodes," and feel that they should try to get rid of them. Nematodes, also important decomposers, are undoubtedly present in large quantities in worm bins, but you would not be likely to see them without a microscope. Under the microscope, nematodes clearly are not made up of segments; they are smooth and round all along their length. Some commercial worm growers are concerned that enchytraeids will compete with redworms for feed, and may attempt to control their numbers. Since the purpose of having a home vermicomposting system is to get rid of food waste, the presence of an organism that helps to do the job is an asset, not a detriment. My position concerning enchytraeids is, "Let them be."

Springtails

In your worm bin, you may see a sprinkling of hundreds of tiny (one-sixteenth inch, 1-3mm) white creatures against the dark background of the decomposing bedding.

 When you put your finger near them, some spring away in all directions. Springtails are primitive wingless insects with a pointed prong extending forward underneath their abdomen from the rear. By quickly extending this "spring," they jump all over the place. Snow fleas are a kind of springtail. Other members in the same group scientists call Collembola do not have the springing tail. Collembola feed on molds and decaying matter. They are important producers of humus and are considered to be among the most important soil organisms.

Springtails are not only numerous, they are diverse, with over 1200 species described. They live in all layers and types of soils from Antarctica to the Arctic, and thrive in moist environments.

Isopods (sowbugs, pill bugs, woodlice, slaters)

Isopods are easy to identify because the series of flattened plates on their bodies makes them look like tiny armadillos. If one of these grey or brown, half-inch (40mm) long creatures rolls up into a ball, it is commonly called a pill bug. Its scientific name is *Armadillidium vulgare*. Sowbugs are related to pill bugs, but don't form little balls. Other common names for isopods are woodlice and, in Australia, slaters.

Isopods are crustaceans, related to crayfish and lobsters. They have gills and need a moist environment for exchange of gases, but they have adapted to life completely on land. The dampness of a worm bin is ideal for them. If you use manure bedding in your worm bin, you are almost certain to have a few isopods grazing over the surface. They won't harm living worms since they eat vegetation and leaf litter, but decaying animal matter is also on their menu.

Centipedes

Centipedes are just about the only critters that I kill on sight in a worm bin. You'll probably never have very many of them, but they are predators that occasionally kill worms. Centipedes move quickly on their many legs and have a pair of poison fangs on the first trunk segment. If you capture a centipede and want to look at it without killing it, immerse the animal briefly in some soda water to let the carbon dioxide anesthetize it.

You can tell a centipede (hundred-legged) from a millipede (thousand-legged) in two ways by looking carefully at their bodies. Centipedes are flattened and have only one pair of legs per segment. Millipedes are cylindrical and have two pairs of legs on each abdominal segment. Both of these segmented creatures are arthropods, not earthworms.

Millipedes

You may find a few millipedes in your worm bin, especially if you use manure, leaf mold, or compost as part of your bedding. They are vegetarians and won't kill your worms. In fact, they are very helpful and contribute more to breaking down organic matter than generally realized. After leaves have been softened by water and bacteria, mil-

lipedes eat holes in them, helping springtails, mites, and other litter dwellers skeletonize them so that only leaf ribs remain. I wouldn't ever consider killing a millipede.

Predatory planarians

Several species of terrestrial planarians prey on earthworms. Planarians are flatworms, or turbellarians. They are normally free-living animals that live in moist places (under rocks, logs, boards, or bricks) rich in organic material. Planarians show no segmentation. Like earthworms, they exchange gases through their moist, mucus-covered skin which may be bright orange or dull yellow with one or more long black stripes. Several inches (70-350mm) long, planarians glide along surfaces with thousands of cilia moving on their ventral surfaces.

A predatory planarian attacks an earthworm by mounting it and attaching a flexible protruding pharynx (feeding tube) to the worm. Digestive juices and secretions from glands in its skin liquefy the worm tissue. The planarian then sucks up the juices through its feeding tube, thereby consuming the earthworm.

It has been reported, but not demonstrated, that earthworm predation by a New Zealand planarian has had a major impact in soil-dwelling earthworm populations in Northern Ireland. Concern exists for other northern European countries because their soil-dwelling earthworms have

not adapted to the introduction of this exotic species and do not have the controls apparently operating in the New Zealand habitat.

During the 1970's, some commercial worm growers in the United States reported predatory planarians attacking worms in their beds. More recently on the Internet I saw one description of a worm associated with worm beds which appeared to be a planarian. I mention predatory planarians here so that more people will be on the alert for them.

Mites

You will undoubtedly have many, many mites in your worm bin. Like the springtails, mites are so small it is diffi-

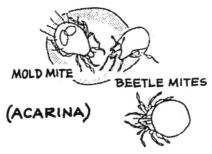

MOLD MITE   BEETLE MITES

(ACARINA)

cult to see them, except as minute dots moving across the surface of the bedding. Mites have eight legs and a round body. Great diversity exists among the tens of thousands of mite species. Some eat plant materials, such as mold, algae, decaying wood, and soft tissues of leaves. Others consume the excrement of other organisms. Beetle mites don't travel very far on their own, but they travel as stowaways on dung beetles, that transport them from one dung heap to another.

One kind of mite, known as the earthworm mite, can be a problem in worm beds. This mite is brown to reddish, and can achieve such high numbers that the worms may refuse to feed. They are more likely to be present in very wet beds, and may concentrate on one or another kind of food, completely covering the surface. If this happens, remove and burn the mite-infested food, or put it out in the sun to kill the mites. Bait others in the same way by placing a piece of bread on the bedding, then remove it when the mites concentrate on its underside.

To create conditions that aren't so favorable for earthworm mites, leave the cover off your bed for a few days to reduce bedding moisture. I have seen only one or two bad infestations of red mites in ten years of using worms to eat my garbage, and I don't consider them a serious problem.

Flies

If someone were to ask me, "What is the most annoying problem you have encountered in having a worm bin in your home?" I would have to answer, "Flies—not odor, not maintenance, not worm crawls, but flies—whether they be fruit flies, fungus gnats, or vinegar flies." Not every box has them, and not every box that has them has them all the time, but when they are present, they are a nuisance.

The flies I am alerting you about are tiny. I don't normally distinguish between fruit and vinegar flies, but the insect books say that fruit flies have greenish, iridescent-colored eyes. Vinegar flies would include *Drosophila* with eyes that are often red or, if we remember our genetics labs, display a range of colors. Fungus gnats and humpbacked flies may live in the worm bin, often seeming to sort of jump and scurry around on the bedding. Such flies are not dangerous. Except for the gnats that bite, they don't bite, sting, or buzz. They undoubtedly come in on fruit peels and rinds, or are attracted by them in late summer or early fall. When food waste is not buried, bin conditions are favorable for their reproduction. Prolific is an apt descriptor. When they land in your orange juice, beer, or champagne, however, they're a bit much. Even the most tolerant guests figure that maybe you've gone too far with this "ecology thing."

To date, I have found no surefire method to get rid of such flies. I prefer not to contaminate my home, the air I breathe, my worms, and my garden with toxic pesticides, so I am not willing to use products that leave harmful residues to eliminate fruit flies. You can do some things, however, to try to lessen their nuisance value.

Prevention

Always bury food waste. If you don't, the odor will bring flies from far and near. They need exposed food to lay eggs. They will do as they were meant to do—lay eggs in a food source for their young. The fly eggs will hatch into

larvae, and the larvae will consume the food source as they go through several larval stages prior to forming a pupa from which will hatch an adult. Fly larvae, or maggots, are quite efficient in breaking down the food waste, but most of us are repulsed by them and would prefer not to see them in our worm bins.

Keep flies away from your storage container. I prefer a screened lid to one that would keep air out of the container because I want oxygen-loving organisms to start the decomposition process from the very start.   If flies are loose in your home, you might place your container in the refrigerator until time to bury the food waste in your worm bin. Some people even freeze the waste.

Friends with compost toilets have suggested getting a cow patty from a field and putting it into the box. Beetles in the cow manure are said to feed on the fly larvae and serve as an effective biological control. Another method described by the compost toilet people is to incorporate a solar-cooking phase to treat all garbage before it is placed in the compost unit. They suggest heating it to the point where fruit flies, eggs, larvae, and pupae will be killed before putting garbage into the bin. Such preventive maintenance might work.

When you deposit food waste in your worm bin, take the time to cover it with a layer (one to two inches, 2-5cm) of bedding. You may need to add some fresh bedding to do this; the additional carbon in the system will be good. Two reasons explain why burying the food waste is necessary. First, the bedding will help to prevent the smell of the food source from reaching the sensitive sensors which all flies have. They will be less likely to know the food source is there. Second, flies are not burrowers. They have no way of burrowing down into the bedding to get to the food sources for laying their eggs. Flies aren't likely to lay eggs on clean newspaper bedding.

Controls

If flies become a problem, try one or more of these remedies:

- Get rid of the adults by trapping, either near the worm bin or food storage area
- Stop feeding the worms for two or three weeks to let the existing larvae pupate and hatch
- Cover food waste with bedding to prevent an other population explosion

(1) The simple trap and attractant described below will attract large numbers of fruit and vinegar flies. This combination doesn't totally get rid of them, but it does keep them somewhat under control. The trap uses several aspects of fly biology to enhance its effectiveness. Flies go toward light, so they travel upwards toward the clear bag on top which traps them inside. Flies are attracted to bright yellow, a color found in many commonly available plastic containers such as mustard jars. Since they feed on yeast, the smell of vinegar, enhanced by a decomposing apple core (or small piece of apple), draws them to the funnel.

To make this trap, use a kitchen knife or scissors to cut off the bottom half of the yellow mustard jar. Poke the bottom corner of a resealable plastic bag into the top of the bottle. Wrap the string tightly around the bag, and tie a knot to secure the bag tightly to the bottle. Then tie the other end of the string, leaving a loop about 10 inches (25cm) long. Pierce the bag and open up the hole so that flies will be able to fly up through the funnel made by the bottle. Tightly close the seal of the bag from the bottom corner up towards the top, letting the double string loop exit through the top corner. Take a break and eat an apple while you plan where you will hang the trap.

Add one tablespoon of apple-cider vinegar to a cup of water and pour this solution into the bag through the hole in the top. Add a piece of apple to the solution. Close the bag as well as you can. Draw the bag up the string to allow some air space above the liquid, and use the clothespin to secure the bag shut around the string. Adjust the bag and its contents so that the attractant doesn't leak out the hole. Hang the bag near your worm bin.

You should find flies in the trap overnight. Empty the trap and change the attractant every week or ten days. At this interval, if the trapped flies lay eggs in the apple, the larvae won't have time to grow up and become adults, too. You can run hot water into the bag to kill any flies and larvae. I could sell you a trap based upon these principles for about $25, but it's more fun to see what you can do with what you can find around the house. I've tried it, and it does work. Materials needed and assembled are shown below:

- The Trap
  - Plastic bag (heavy-duty, resealable)
  - String (24 inches, 60cm)
  - Yellow plastic container (mustard jar)
  - Clothes pin or spring-clip
- The Attractant
  - Apple-cider vinegar
  - Apple core

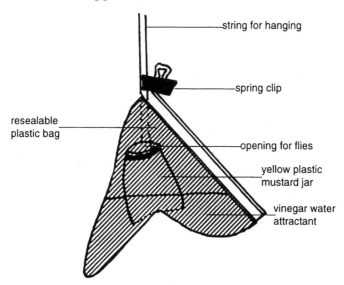

Figure 28. Homemade traps are effective.

(2) Biological controls may work. People have reported some success adding beneficial nematodes to their worm

bin. Available from some garden supply catalogs, these nematodes drill into and consume fly larvae and pupae in the worm bin. Used in conjunction with a trap and attractant to reduce the adult fly population, application of beneficial nematodes to the bin may do the trick.

A recent suggestion which I have not yet tried came from K.P. Plater who has used worms to eat his garbage for 45 years. He came upon this possible solution to the fruit fly problem after tens of thousands of ladybugs invaded Bucks County, Pennsylvania, during the summer of 1996. In the spring of 1997, hundreds of ladybugs were on all windows of his home. He captured a handful and placed them underneath the plastic cover on his worm bin. He was delighted to report that he is now completely free of fruit flies! Mr. Plater acknowledges that it may have been accidental, and further experimentation may be necessary, but at 88 years old, he says he is too old for further trials. Ladybugs are certainly worth a try!

Disposal

Although this method deserves a minus from the standpoint of environmental soundness because it requires electricity, if you get desperate, suck up flies with a vacuum cleaner. When I lift the lid on my box and lots of fruit flies fly up and land on the basement ceiling, my vacuum cleaner just inhales them. Although not a complete control, this method does help to cut down the numbers.

Other suggestions

I recommend adding a cup or so of rock dust to a worm bin perhaps twice a year. This by-product from the gravel and rock-crushing industry is gaining in popularity with those who feel that our soils are severely lacking in trace minerals from excessive agricultural activity. They claim that not only will rock dust provide many trace minerals to make the vermicompost from a worm bin far more nutritious for plants, it will help balance the worm bin environment so that flies will be less of a problem.

Diatomaceous earth sprinkled on the surface of the bedding hasn't worked. Yellow plastic discs covered with mineral oil or honey to attract and hold flies have worked to a certain extent. A stickier adhesive might work better.

Ants

I have never had a problem with ants in my vermicomposting bin, but then I don't have a problem with ants in my home, either. In milder climates, though, ants could be a problem for which controls must be sought.

A paste of borax and sugar mixed with a little water is an effective control for ants, but harmless to people. Setting up physical barriers to prevent their access is also possible. For example, I would set the legs of my worm bin in coffee cans with mineral oil in the bottom. The ants would get trapped in the oil and would not be able to enter the bin. Or, I might try dabbing Vaseline on a piece of cotton and making a continuous one-inch (2.5cm) swath around the top of my worm bin. I would try these measures before resorting to commercial ant baits that use arsenic as their primary killing agent.

Disease organisms

A question sometimes asked is, "Can you get viruses, germs, or diseases from your worm bin?" That's not a simple question to answer. I have already discussed the potential for transmitting toxoplasmosis if cats are allowed to use a worm bin as a litter box. The organism for this disease is known to pass intact through the digestive tract of an earthworm.

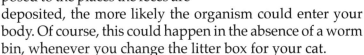

If your cat is harboring the organism, it can pass into the cat's feces. The more you are exposed to the places the feces are deposited, the more likely the organism could enter your body. Of course, this could happen in the absence of a worm bin, whenever you change the litter box for your cat.

For similar reasons I discourage people from even considering using worm bins as described in this book for treating human manure. Pathogens (disease-producing organisms) can be transmitted in human manure. Our complex and increasingly expensive wastewater treatment facilities are designed to reduce or eliminate the possibility that these organisms will reach our soils and water supplies. Although high-temperature composting has been shown to be effective in killing pathogens, home vermicomposting systems do not generate the high temperatures characteristic of well-constructed, large-mass, compost heaps.

Some research suggests that passage through an earthworm's gut can reduce the number of pathogens present in sewage sludges. This is preliminary work, and more research needs to be done in this area. Until solid data are available, caution against using human waste is in order unless it is in a composting system designed for human waste which uses worms to enhance its effectiveness.

One further caution—if you are overly sensitive or allergic to fungi and mold spores, you probably won't be able to have a worm bin in your home. Molds can and do develop in natural succession during the composting process. You may have to reserve your vermicomposting activities for outdoor locations, perhaps with someone else doing the required maintenance. Another possibility would be to keep your bin acidity within a pH range of six to eight, outside the optimal range for fungi (pH4 to 6).

CRITTER SUMMARY

You are likely to find many organisms other than earthworms in your worm bin. In truth, the system won't work if they aren't present. Your worm culture is not a monoculture. Instead, it is a diverse, interdependent community of large and small organisms. No one species can possibly overtake all the other species present. They serve as food for each other, clean up each others' debris, convert materials to forms that others can utilize, and control each others' populations. Soils with high organic content are likely to contain great numbers of soil organisms. Since the nature of vermicompost is basically organic, no one should be surprised that it also contains soil organisms in great variety and large numbers.

For us to arbitrarily decide who should live and who should die in this complex system is a bit presumptuous. Although some controls are suggested, this chapter's major purpose is to provide a better idea of what you can expect to find. Don't be alarmed at what you see. Information tempers fear. You may even decide to learn more about those critters that you once used to squash when you found them.

13
How do plants benefit from a worm bin?

COMPLETING THE CIRCLE

From the beginning, I have tried to relate having worms eat your garbage to having healthier plants. This happens when you use the vermicompost from your worm bin on your house plants and gardens. What is the nature of this rich humus, and how should you use it?

It helps to remember the distinction between worm castings and vermicompost. Worm castings are deposits that once moved through the digestive tract of a worm. Vermicompost is a dark mixture of worm castings, organic material, and bedding in varying stages of decomposition, plus the living earthworms, cocoons, and other organisms present.

If you choose a low-maintenance system, a large proportion of your vermicompost will be worm castings. A worm casting (also known as worm cast or vermicast) is a biologically active mass containing thousands of bacteria, enzymes, and remnants of plant materials and animal manures that were not digested by the earthworm. The composting process continues after a worm casting has been deposited. In fact, the bacterial population of a cast is much greater than the bacterial population of either ingested soil or the earthworm's gut.

An important component of vermicompost is humus. Humus is a complex material formed during the breakdown of organic matter. One of its components, humic acid, provides many binding sites for plant nutrients, such as calcium, iron, potassium, sulfur and phosphorus. These nutrients are stored in the humic acid molecule in a form readily available to plants, and are released when the plants require them. Humus increases the aggregation of soil particles which, in turn, enhances permeability of the soil to water and air. It also buffers the soil, reducing the detrimental effects of excessively acid or alkaline soils. Humus has also been shown to stimulate plant growth and to exert a beneficial control on plant pathogens, harmful fungi, nematodes, and harmful bacteria. One of the basic tenets of gardening organically is to carry out procedures that increase the humus component of the soil; earthworm activity certainly does this.

How to use vermicompost

You will have several buckets full of vermicompost from your worm bin. Use it selectively and sparingly. Vermicompost is loaded with humus, worm castings, and decomposing matter. The cocoons and worms present are unlikely to survive long outside the comfort of your bin. Plant nutrients will be present, both in stored and immediately available forms. Vermicompost in sufficient quantities also helps to hold moisture in the soil, which is an added advantage during dry periods.

Seed beds

Vermicompost will not "burn" your plants as some commercial fertilizers do, but since your supply will be limited, use it only where it will do the most good. One method is to prepare your seed row with a hoe, making a shallow, narrow trench. Sprinkle vermicompost into the seed row. In this way, the new seeds will have the vermicompost as a rich source of nutrients soon after they germinate and during early stages of their growth.

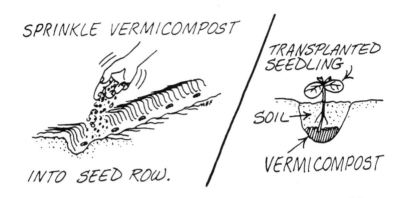

Figure 29. Seeds and young plants benefit from nutrients present in vermicompost.

Transplants

For transplanting such favorites as cabbage, broccoli, and tomatoes, which are usually set out in the garden as young plants, throw a handful of vermicompost in the bottom of each hole you dig for a plant. Don't worry if worms or cocoons are present in the vermicompost. While the worms are alive, they will produce castings and add nitrogen from their mucus, but they are not likely to do all the other good things that worms do for the soil. Also, don't expect your redworms to thrive in your garden. They are not normally a soil-dwelling worm, and require large amounts of organic material to live. If you were to add large quantities of manure, leaves, or other organic material, you might get a few *Eisenia fetida* to live, but most will probably die. When they do, their bodies will add needed nitrogen to the soil, so all is not lost! Hopefully, your gardening techniques will improve the organic matter concentrations in your garden so that the soil-dwelling species of earthworms will be fruitful and multiply.

Top dressing

You will use most of the supply of vermicompost from your winter's production during spring planting. Any remaining can be used later in the season as top or side dressing. At this time you won't want to disturb the root systems, but it is a simple matter to sprinkle vermicompost around the base and drip line of your plants, giving them an additional supply of nutrients, providing organic matter, and enabling the mid-season plants to benefit from vermicompost's water-holding capacity.

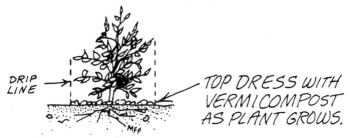

DRIP LINE

TOP DRESS WITH VERMICOMPOST AS PLANT GROWS.

Figure 30. Nutrients become available to plants when water drips from thier leaves onto vermicompost placed around the base of each plant.

How to use worm castings

After several months of low-maintenance technique, the contents of the worm bin will be dark and smell like earth, a crumbly material. Since little food is left in this material for earthworms, very few worms will be present. Populations of active microorganisms will also have dwindled; those present will be in a dormant state awaiting reactivation in a suitable environment of new food and moisture.

Except for some large chunks, most of this worm-bin material is worm castings. Worm castings differ from vermicompost in being more homogeneous, with few pieces of recognizable bedding or food waste. When dried and screened, castings look so much like plain, black organic topsoil that you may be surprised to recall that little or no soil went into the original bedding.

While some drying of worm castings is desirable, it is best not to let them dry to the point when they become powdery, for it then becomes difficult to wet them down. They may even form a crust on the surface and slow water penetration. Worm castings with about 25-35% moisture have a good, crumbly texture and earthy smell, and are just about right to use on your plants.

Chemistry and castings

Although pure worm castings provide many nutrients for plants in a form the plants can use as needed, some precautions should be taken in their use. The organic material present in food waste is likely to have been broken down to a greater extent in worm castings than in vermicompost. More carbon will have been oxidized and given off as car-

Figure 31. Different potting media affect the health of African violets.

bon dioxide, leaving nitrogen, phosphorus, potassium, calcium, and other elements to combine to form various salts.

High concentrations of some salts can inhibit plant growth. They may not be a "complete" fertilizer for some plants. Often having a pH8 or higher, worm castings may not be suitable for acid-loving plants. Worm castings should be mixed with other potting materials. In this way, plants gain the advantage of the nutrients present without suffering from excessive salt concentrations.

An intriguing experiment, which seems to verify the need to dilute pure castings, was conducted by a horticulturist at the Kalamazoo Nature Center in the 1970's. Three sets of African violet plants were potted, each set in a different medium (see Figure 31). The plants on the left, labeled PS, grew in 100% potting soil; C (right), 100% worm castings; and C-P-MP (center), equal amounts of worm castings, perlite, and Michigan peat. If you compare the plants grown in potting soil with those grown in worm castings note that the castings-grown plants look healthier. Those grown in the potting soil show **chlorosis** (yellowing) of some leaves, a sign of possible nutrient deficiency.

The center row of plants, grown with worm castings diluted with perlite and peat, was distinctly more vigorous than either of the other two sets of plants. Leaves were larger, greener, and more robust. A likely interpretation of this experiment is that, although the 100% castings provided more nutrients for the young plants than the potting soil, salt concentrations in the castings may have been great enough to inhibit their growth. The center row of plants had the benefit of nutrients from the castings, but was not inhibited by too high a concentration of salts, since the concentration had been reduced by dilution with the perlite and peat.

Of course, other interpretations are possible. For example, the center row of plants may have had an advantage contributed by the water-holding capacity of the peat, plus the increased lightness of the potting mixture due to the perlite. Further experiments could discriminate between these possibilities, but from this preliminary work, it seems safe to say that some castings are better than no castings, and pure castings may not be as good as other possible mixes.

In the 1980's, Dr. Clive Edwards, now of Ohio State University, led a team of scientists who conducted extensive plant growth studies that compared worm castings to commercial potting media in his native England. Castings were produced by worms working on a variety of wastes, such as cattle and pig manures, brewery waste, and potato waste. Although adding magnesium and adjusting pH to decrease alkalinity were sometimes necessary, media containing worm castings produced plants with as good or better seed germination, plant growth, and earlier flowering. This was true even when worm castings comprised as little as 5% of the mixture. Other more recent work supports these findings. Dr. Edwards and others speculate that worm castings may contain substances which work as hormones to support plant growth.

Investigations are underway to refine this knowledge further. As scientific and commercial development of vermicomposting proceeds, the true economic value of worm castings will become apparent. In the meantime your plants certainly will benefit from the castings the worms in your worm bin produce.

To sterilize or not to sterilize

Some people suggest "sterilizing" potting mixes and/or worm castings, prior to use in house plants and greenhouses, to kill organisms that could cause the plants trouble

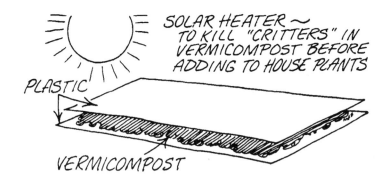

SOLAR HEATER ~
TO KILL "CRITTERS" IN
VERMICOMPOST BEFORE
ADDING TO HOUSE PLANTS

PLASTIC

VERMICOMPOST

in a confined environment. The term "sterilizing" is being used loosely here, since the dictionary definition of sterilization literally is "the destruction of all living microorganisms, as pathogenic or saprophytic bacteria, vegetative forms, and spores." Surgical instruments, for example, are sterilized in an autoclave under high temperature and pressure for a specified period of time. For our purposes, it would be more correct to say that potting soil is pasteurized; that is, it is exposed to a high temperature or poisonous gas for a long enough period of time to kill certain microorganisms, but not all. In any case, whether you prefer to call it sterilize or pasteurize, I don't recommend that you do either to worm castings. Soil (vermicompost) is a dynamic, living entity, and much of its value comes from the millions of microorganisms present.

One concern many people have about using worm castings directly on their house plants is, "Won't those little white worms and all those bugs I can see crawling around hurt my plants?" Probably not. The enchytraeids eat dead and decaying material, not living plants, and so do the mites and springtails that are likely to still be present when your vermicompost is almost all worm castings. The organisms that thrived in your worm box are not likely to be the kind that also attack living plants. If there are just a few, don't worry about them.

There may be a lot. If you have a true aversion to having visible critters in the worm castings you want to sprinkle under your plants, place your worm castings on a sheet of plastic outdoors in the sun. Put another sheet of plastic on top, and let this "solar heater" warm things up a bit. Most of the white worms will move onto the plastic, and most of the mites and springtails will be killed from the heat. Collect your castings in a few hours. They will be ready to use in potting mixes, as top dressing, or in your garden.

Potting mixes

Worm castings may be mixed with various concentrations of potting materials, such as peat moss, sand, topsoil, perlite, vermiculite, or leaf mold. One satisfactory mix of equal parts by volume has these ingredients:

1/4 worm castings...............for nutrients
1/4 peat moss.......................for moisture retention
1/4 perlite............................for aeration
1/4 sand or garden soil.......for body

Experiment with different mixes, and find the ones that suit your favorite plants.

Soil blocks

A device called a "soil blocker" can make a few worm castings go a long way. This small, hand-operated machine made of plastic or metal enables you to compress a potting soil mixture into a 2x2x3-inch (5 x 5 x 7.5cm) block in which you plant seeds. Make up a wetter than normal potting mix containing about 25% worm castings, and compress it into the block of soil. Plant a seed in this block; keep it moist, as you would a peat pot. When the young plant is ready to transplant, insert the soil block into its hole and the young plant will take off without undergoing the normal transplant shock.

Top dressing

Sprinkle worm castings about one-fourth inch (6mm) deep on the soil surface that supports your potted plants, and water as usual. Repeat every 45 to 60 days. If necessary, remove some of the soil above the roots so that you have room for the worm castings. Let excess water move through the soil occasionally to flush out accumulations of salts,

USE CASTINGS TO TOP DRESS HOUSE PLANTS.

REPEAT EVERY 45~60 DAYS.

TAKE OUT 1/4 INCH OF SOIL TO ALLOW ROOM FOR CASTINGS.

particularly if you have hard water. And remember, don't use softened water on your plants; it contains other salts that do harm.

In your garden, sprinkle worm castings along the bottom of your seed row or throw a handful of castings into the hole at the time you are transplanting. The adjacent soil will dilute excessive salt concentrations in the castings. It is perfectly natural for vegetable seeds present in the vermicompost to sprout. Simply pull these sprouts as you would pull weeds.

AN ADDED BONUS

Have you ever tried to germinate an avocado pit? Have you tried the trick with the three toothpicks, inserting them around the diameter of the pit, placing it on top of a jar of water, and keeping it watered for ... well, months? Until you either got tired of it, or it finally did sprout?

Well, have I got a deal for you! Throw your pits into your worm bin, cover, and forget about them. That's all. In time—it may take months, but be patient—you will find a taproot coming out of the bottom, and a sprout coming out of the top. When this happens, transfer it to a pot. One winter, nine out of ten avocado pits I tried this way germinated. I now have more avocado plants than I know what to do with—in the living room, on the front porch, on the side porch, in my office. . . . You, too, can be the first on your block to be a success with your sprouted avocado pits.

14.
How can I treat
waste as a resource?

The process of recycling returns materials to a previous stage in a repetitive process. In a natural ecosystem the wastes from one process become the resources for other processes, a concept discussed earlier in Chapter 12. In other words, there is no waste in nature, but a continuous flow of materials and energy from one organism to another through basic cycles such as the carbon, nitrogen, or water cycle.

Our current industrial society treats waste as something to throw away, to get rid of, to dispose of. We need to change the way we think about waste. We need to think, "Waste is a resource. Resources have value." And we need to ask ourselves, "How can we move from a waste**ful** society to a waste-**free** society?" Canberra, Australia's capital city, is the world's first community to establish the goal, "No waste by 2010." For its citizens and governmental leaders, a waste-free society is one in which no material is regarded as useless, where all resources find another application or useful function. Environmental activists in the United States are more likely to use the term "Zero Waste" in the place of "waste free," but both terms represent the same concept.

Zero Waste and worms

Worm bins could contribute significantly to achieving the goal of a waste-free or zero-waste society. Food residues turn into plant nutrients through the action of worms.

A big advantage of worm bins is that this recycling takes place on-site, close to (if not in) people's homes. People are willing to have worm bins because they can eliminate smelly kitchen wastebaskets. Trash containers will less likely attract flies; lifting their lids won't cause people to reel from the fumes. I've often said, "The time to publicize a worm-composting program is three weeks into a garbage haulers' strike in a city like Philadelphia!"

With a worm bin in your home, you will find it more pleasant to examine some of the materials you throw away. Think about where they go. Can more of those materials be recycled? Aren't we going to run out of raw materials if we just keep throwing things away after using them? Can you come closer to having a zero-waste household?

Fortunately, many more citizens have access to recycling programs than they did in the early 1980's when the first edition of this book came out. At that time, only about 700 communities had curbside recycling programs. In 1996, citizens in nearly 9000 cities could participate in recycling just by taking their recyclables to the curb. Recycling has become so commonplace that over 100 million people in the United States recycle. According to the Grassroots Recycling Network, more people recycle than vote!

Why has the public embraced recycling so wholeheartedly? People sense the practicality of the old adage, "Waste not, want not." Recycling saves materials by turning them back into valuable products rather than burning them in an incinerator or burying them in a landfill. Recycling also creates jobs. It redistributes wealth. Sorting and processing recyclables provides five to ten times more jobs than landfilling or incineration. The cost to build recycling processing facilities is much less than the capital investment required for an incinerator or landfill. For another thing, recycling saves energy. It takes about 6% of the energy to recycle the aluminum in a pop can than to produce that aluminum from bauxite.

Have we gone far enough? No. Do all of your plastic milk jugs get turned into permanent, high-quality park benches? What about your wine bottles? Do they get rewashed, sterilized, and reused? What about the juice containers that are made from multiple materials—paper, plastic, aluminum? Have you found anyplace where you can recycle them? What about the diapers that go to the landfill?

Obviously, we have a long way to go to achieve a zero-waste society. Here are some things you can do:

THE THREE R'S

Reduce

Reduce the amount of materials that flow into and out of your home. Buy for quality and longevity when possible. Repair when you can and, through your buying habits, encourage production of products that can be repaired. Refuse excess packaging by buying items that have less packaging.

American society does not make it easy to reduce materials consumption. We are told that economic indicators for a healthy U.S. economy depend on spending to acquire more stuff that others produce. If no one buys, the demand for production and jobs falls. Less money changes hands, and fewer people have money to spend. A vicious circle, indeed. Money spent on stuff no one needs, however, could be saved and used for more positive purposes. "Reduce" saves money as well as materials.

Reuse

Reuse what you can—plastic bags, jars, boxes. Plastic milk jugs can be used to store soft, non-chlorinated rainwater for watering your house plants. Nails can be pulled from scrap lumber; both can be reused for building projects. Save your charcoal for another cookout by pouring water over the coals when you have taken the food off your grill. Develop a conservation mentality (some people might say, "Depression mindset," referring to the tenor of the early 1930's) about the use of materials.

What you think about what you do determines your attitude. Attitude, of course, is a little thing that makes a big difference. Thinking stewardship feels better than thinking deprivation. The better you feel about your behaviors, the longer you'll be willing to maintain them. People have shared with me that composting their garbage with worms makes them feel good. They like turning the most repulsive part of their garbage into something useful. Let companies know what you think. You can find their addresses and names of their managers by visiting or calling your public library. Encourage production of packaging that can be reused and recycled, rather than mixtures of plastics and paper which are not good for either reuse or recycling.

Recycle

Recycle all of your newspapers, cans, glass, and aluminum. As the cost of obtaining virgin materials increases, incentives for recycling already-processed materials also increase, creating larger and more reliable markets for recycled materials.

The road is not always smooth, however. One example comes from the paper industry. Many programs for collecting paper came on-line before sufficient paper-mill capacity was available to process it. Prices for recycled paper fell. Communities couldn't get rid of the paper they had collected. Some of it ended up in landfills. But mechanisms were in place to correct the situation. Governmental mandates required that the paper purchased by federal agencies have a minimum content of recycled paper. This huge market helped make decision-makers and financiers confident that they could sell paper with recycled content if they invested in new mills. Mills with tremendous capacity to process paper came on-line. By 1995, 48% of office paper was being recycled, and the paper industry has established a new goal of 65% by 2000. The new mills will have such tremendous capacity to process post-consumer paper they will require massive levels of recycling to obtain enough feedstock for producing recycled paper.

During the next decade, more kinds of materials will be sought for recycling programs. Categories recoverable by some combination of current technologies are plant debris, metals, glass, ceramics, soils, wood, textiles, putrescibles, reusable goods, and paper. Every one of the recoverable categories is being processed by hundreds of companies. Note that plastics and chemicals are not in this list. Because some materials may be so difficult to recover in ways that are environmentally sound, financial disincentives (penalties) are possibilities to reduce their use.

Both economic and political forces influence the direction of these programs. You can help by striving for environmentally-sound programs, not only in your own home, but in your community. While the preceding ideas and those that follow are somewhat general, they are based on environmental priorities for people who are aware of human impacts on our planet. They are appropriate suggestions for moving away from our consumer orientation towards one of living gently on the Earth.

If you are not already recycling, here are some tips to help you get started. They may help you keep waste-disposal costs down and acknowledge your role as caretaker.

Paper products

It's not unusual to generate 20 to 30 shopping bags of newspapers, junkmail, and paperboard packaging every three to four months. Separate contaminants, such as carbon paper, plastic, plastic windows on envelopes, filament tape, from the load you put on the curb. Wire staples can stay because they are removed by magnets during processing.

Materials preparation

Each one of nearly 9000 curbside recycling programs has its own requirements for material preparation. However, it is very likely that all of them ask you to remove paper labels from cans and flatten them when possible to save storage space. When you finally send the glass jars you can no longer reuse out for recycling, you won't need to remove their labels because the paper burns away when the glass is remelted. Plastic containers should be rinsed and lids removed. Lids are made from a different type of plastic, and contaminate the lot when present. Programs for collecting clean plastic bags and Styrofoam exist in some communities. Mixed paper and plastic packaging still contribute more to the volume of municipal trash than I like. As long as plastic is considered cheap and disposable, zero waste will be difficult to achieve.

Food waste

Because worms eat my garbage, thereby eliminating the materials that make the odor from mixed trash unbearable, the plastic bags in which I store trash are neither unpleasant nor an attraction for varmints. I stockpile them in my garage, and make a dump run only three to four times a year. The zero waste goal would be to reduce this quantity of material to zero.

Worms are the key to this system. Organic waste isn't mixed with the trash. The transfer station I use does not accept food waste from residents who haul their own trash, anyway. If I didn't have worms processing my garbage, I would have to pay extra for residential pickup by private haulers. That I have a suitable vehicle and space to stockpile it helps.

MONEY-SAVING OPTIONS

Other ways to benefit financially by using worms to process kitchen waste depend upon the collection/disposal options in your own community. Two possibilities follow:

Purchase tagged bags

In some communities, residents pay for color-coded trash bags set out as necessary for weekly pickup. This method provides an incentive for lowering the volume of residential trash since the fewer bags put out, the fewer you pay for. One woman who installed a home vermicompost-ing system found that, instead of placing a trash bag at the curb every week, she could wait three weeks before it was necessary The difference wasn't the reduced volume of trash—without organic waste in the bag, she could tolerate the odor when opening it to deposit waste over a longer period of time.

Ask for rates tied to use

Differential rates for trash pickup are becoming more common. With such systems every family who normally uses three garbage cans per week could cut back to one can per week if it installs a home vermicomposting system and recycles all recyclables. This possibility may not exist in your area because of garbage-collection practices. However, money could be saved to be available for other things when municipalities and waste-disposal firms do the right thing. Landfills will last longer. Toxic leachates are less likely to develop since organic acids from the garbage will not be produced to react with metals and other materials in the dump. Libraries, community centers, parks and recreation services could be supported with money now used for land-fills. Families could pay less for garden fertilizer, less to purchase fishing bait, and . . . and . . . and . . . . Why isn't everybody doing it?

SUMMARY

Earthworms in nature play an important role in recy-cling organic nutrients from dead tissues back into living organisms. They do this without fanfare; rarely does any-one see them perform their tasks.

If you decide to use composting worms to process your own organic kitchen waste, you will see them at work. You will see mounds of disagreeable material converted noise-lessly, with almost no odor, to materials you can use directly on your house plants and in your garden. You will enjoy healthier looking plants, better tasting vegetables, and money in the bank. You will spend less on fertilizers and trash disposal. Some of you will have fish on the table, enticed by "your" worms that attracted them as bait. Hopefully, you'll also gain a better appreciation of the intricate balance and interdependencies in nature. You will be treading more gently upon the Earth.

As your gardens are enriched, so is your life and mine. You will have joined the worm-working adventurers who say, "Worms eat my garbage." Isn't that a grand beginning on a task that needs to start somewhere? You, personally, can make it happen.

Afterword:
How many worms in an acre?*

One year I counted and weighed all the earthworms I could hand sort from the top seven inches of a square foot dug from my garden's soil. I counted 62 worms of all sizes, and found at least two species. If I had had an acre under cultivation and if this were, in fact, a representative sample, the total population would have exceeded 2.7 million worms per acre!

These 62 worms weighed two ounces. Extended to one acre, this would give a total weight of 5445 pounds, or over two and one-half tons of worms in the top seven inches of one acre (43,560 sq ft) of soil!

How much do their castings weigh?

Earthworms of the soil-dwelling type eat soil in their search for organic nutrients. They mix the soil with organic materials and bacteria in their intestines, and excrete the mixed deposit as castings. The weight of these castings per worm per day could easily equal the weight of the worm. Let's estimate conservatively that the weight of castings deposited per day from one worm is one-eighth the worm's weight. The total weight of castings produced per acre per day would be 680 pounds. Think of the worm's activity in producing those castings and their value to plants.

To estimate annual casting production, let's assume that the worms are active only 150 days of the year, giving 102,093 pounds per acre per year, or over 51 tons of castings per year. (If you have ever tossed a ton of manure onto a pickup truck and off again, you can begin to appreciate the work worms do for you in your garden.) Charles Darwin's approach in 1881 to estimating castings production was to

*Metric conversions for these quantities and areas are approximate, for reasons developed further in Appendix C: "A metric scenario."

collect, dry, and weigh all castings from a square yard of grass for a whole year. He recorded from three to 16 tons of dry earth annually ejected by worms in the form of castings.

How do agricultural practices affect earthworms?

Some modern agricultural practices have not only reduced soil earthworm and microbial populations, but also the amounts of organic matter present in the soil. Less organic matter results in less food for worms. In addition, plowing and tilling not only kills worms directly, but exposes them to predators and drying conditions. Worm burrows provide a means for water to move deeper into the soil. Plowing destroys worm burrows, reducing the capacity of the soil to hold water and increasing the possibility of flooding during torrential rains.

Crop management practices which result in increased worm populations have also demonstrated higher crop yields. Such practices include less tillage, planting cover crops, and retaining stubble, all methods that retain moisture and provide food for the worms. An example reported by John Buckerfield from Australia showed substantial grape yield increases when straw mulch and composted yard trimmings were applied underneath the vines. The increase in crop yield correlated with increased earthworm populations. Other promising research showed that applying vermicomposted grape residue and cattle manure to vineyards and other horticultural crops increased yields. Applied under mulch, these applications also reduced the need for irrigation and weed control.

Apparently, many climatic regions could benefit from applying this knowledge related to earthworms, whether they be earthworkers or vermicomposters. Part of my work is to help people understand how earthworms enhance the quality of our soils, our food, and our lives. I also want to discourage those practices that kill these amazing creatures. Their production of natural manure has been creating and improving soils for millions of years.

Appendix A:
Record sheet

Date set up_____= Day 0

Description of set-up:
Initial weight of worms_____
❑ Breeders or ❑ mixed sizes
Type of bedding_____
Size of bin_____
Number in household_____
Garbage burying locations:

	2'		3'
2'	1 6 7 2 5 8 3 4 9	2'	1 6 7 12 2 5 8 11 3 4 9 10

Date	Day	# oz.	Total # oz. to date	Temp.	Water # of pints	Burying location #	Comments

Date harvested_____No. of Days_____Worm wgt._____
Total wgt. garbage buried_____oz. =_____lb.
Wgt. uneaten garbage_____
Ave. oz. buried per day_____
Ave temp._____ Temp. range_____

Appendix B:
Annotated references

Earthworm books for the layperson

Brown, Amy. *Earthworms in New Zealand*. Auckland, New Zealand: Reed Publishing Ltd., 39 Rawene Road, Birkenhead, Auckland. 1995. 110p

A gem of a book written by the late Amy Brown. This writer turned to worm-farmer and back to writer when she realized how much her passion for worms was consuming her life. "New Zealand" in the title is far too limiting for this book which describes the major composting worms (*Eisenia fetida* and *Lumbricus rubellus)* and earthworms which are most likely to influence soil structure and fertility when present in sufficient numbers. She reports on the excellent work done in New Zealand by its soil scientists. They correlate agricultural management practices which enhance earthworm populations with the ability to support one or two more cows or sheep per acre of pasture because of increased vegetation.

Ernst, David. *The Farmer's Earthworm Handbook: Managing Your Underground Money-makers*. Brookfield, WI: Lessiter Publications, P.O. Box 624, Brookfield, WI 53008-0624. 1995. 112p

David Ernst gives us a practical, well-researched book written by an obvious worm enthusiast. He goes to the scientific literature for documentation on the effects of earthworms on agricultural crops. Farmers share their experiences switching from conventional tillage practices which reduce earthworm populations to those which allow the earthworm populations to come back. Ernst presents information on identification of common earthworkers, tillage practices, manure management, chemical effects on earthworms, and cover crops.

Hopp, Henry. *What Every Gardener Should Know About Earthworms.* Pownal, VT: Storey Communications, 1973. 39p
Although much of the information in this meaty little booklet was adapted from a 1954 publication entitled *Let An Earthworm Be Your Garbage Man*, the presentation on effects of earthworms on soil moisture, aeration, and soil fertility is still pertinent.

Edwards, Ray. *The Nightcrawler Manual*, 5th edition. Eagle River, WI: Shields Publications, P.O. Box 699, Eagle River, WI. 1990, 1976. 144p
This manual is one of few which gives information about keeping—not breeding—nightcrawlers. Edwards, who has studied nightcrawlers for years, tells how to harvest, hold, feed, water, and condition them for fishing. Breeding nightcrawlers (*Lumbricus terrestris*) is not practical because of their burrowing behavior and requirement for large volumes of soil to inhabit.

Earthworm books for the advanced student

Edwards, C.A. and P.J. Bohlen. *Biology and Ecology of Earthworms*, 3rd edition. London, England: Chapman and Hall, 1996. 426p
This newly-revised text covers morphology, taxonomy, biology, physiology, ecology, the role of earthworms in organic matter cycles, and other subjects related to earthworms. Technical, but with a wealth of interesting information, it was written by scientists currently conducting earthworm research. This book is a must for serious students of earthworms.

Appelhof, Mary (compiler). *Workshop on the Role of Earthworm in the Stabilization of Organic Residues. Vol. 1: Proceedings.* Kalamazoo, MI: Beech Leaf Press, 1981. 340p

World's leading investigators of earthworm reviewed pertinent information and projected future research needed to develop the potential for organic waste conversion by means of earthworms. Supported by the National Science Foundation, this document provided the stimulus for subsequent work in applied vermiculture. Its companion, *Vol. II: Bibliography,* compiled and edited by Diane D. Worden in 1981, 492p, provides access to 3036 journal articles, books, patents, dissertations, and federally-supported research in the decade prior to 1981.

Edwards, C.A. and Edward F. Newhauser (eds). *Earthworms in Waste and Environmental Management.* The Hague, Netherlands: SPB Academic Publ BV, 1988. 392p

This book includes papers presented at the First International Conference on Earthworms in Waste and Environmental Management held in Cambridge, England. More than any other single document, it reports on laboratory and large-scale trials of the application of earthworms in waste management, land reclamation, the production of horticultural potting media, and as bioindicators of soil contamination by chemicals. A basic resource for anyone considering going into large-scale vermiculture.

Earthworm farming

Brown, Amy. *Earthworms Unlimited.* Kenthurst, Australia: 3 Whitehall Road, Kenthurst, New South Wales 2156. 1994. 80p

A long-standing fascination for worms and the idea of setting up a potential source of income for a relative stimulated Amy Brown to collect 1400 worms from a compost pile. She used information from the basic worm growers' manuals and her own experience to sort out types of bins, bedding, feeds, procedures, packaging, and marketing aspects of worm growing. She convinced herself that a viable business could be developed, but sold her experimental worm farm so that she could go back to her full-time profession of writing. She shares the knowledge she gained in a humorous, informative manner and provides in one little book what would take several other books to uncover.

Barrett, Thomas J. *Harnessing the Earthworms.* Wedgwood Press. Available from Shields Publications, P.O. Box 699, Eagle River, WI. 1947, 1959. 166p
Frustrating because it lacks a bibliography, this important document synthesizes much of the early literature on the effects of earthworms on soil fertility. Discusses humus, topsoil, subsoil, earthworm tillage, and chemical composition of earthworms castings. Excellent and still useful information on earthworm culture is provided.

Shields, Earl B. *Raising Earthworms for Profit,* 19th edition. Eagle River, WI: Shields Publications, P.O. Box 699, Eagle River, WI. 1994, 1959. 128p
This manual has been the standard training manual for hundreds, if not thousands, of worm growers. It discusses markets, propagation boxes, indoor and outdoor pits, feeds, packing and shipping, and advertising. The basic text was written in the 1950's.

Holcombe, Dan and John J. Longfellow. *Oregon Soil Corporation Reactor: Blueprint for a Successful Vermiculture Compost System.* Bend, OR: Recyclit Corporation, 63415 Saddleback Drive, Bend, OR 97701. 1995. 54p
This manual provides construction details and operation procedures for a self-harvesting vermicomposting unit made of wood. The OSCR system is based

upon the successful large-scale vermicomposting reactor Holcombe operates to process several tons of
organic waste per day. Each modular unit can process from 6 to 12 pounds (2.7-5.5kg) food waste daily
depending on whether worms are working under
optimal conditions of food, air, moisture, and temperature. Of particular value are the 12 tables giving
information about bin capacity, cost, income/expense
estimates, return on investment for schools, parts lists
and cost estimates for used wood versus new wood,
testing and support tools, carbon/nitrogen ratios, and
castings analyses. A project manager with access to
this manual would save hours of calculations while
writing a proposal for an institutional vermicomposting system.

Bogdanov, Peter. *Commercial Vermiculture: How to Build
a Thriving Business in Redworms.* Merlin, OR: Vermico, P.O.
Box 1134, Merlin, OR 97532. 1996. 88p
    With its focus on how to make money raising earth-
worms, this new book is a welcome source of up-to-
date information on the business of vermiculture.
Bogdanov puts vermiculture into a historical context,
gives basic information about composting worms,
tells how to get started, and describes how to set up
commercial beds. He covers pests and predators, harvesting, and packaging and shipping. This book is a
must for anyone wanting to go into the worm business.

Composting

Dindal, Daniel L. *Ecology of Compost: A Public Involvement Project.* Syracuse, NY: State University of New York
College of Environmental Science and Forestry, 1972. 12p
    A soil ecologist presents a primer on outdoor com-
posting. Dindal discusses energy sources, decomposition rates, the carbon-nitrogen ratio, moisture, aera-

tion, and heat production. He described the relationships between the organisms found in "Food Web of the Compost Pile" which is used in this book.

Martin, Deborah L. and Grace Gershuny (eds.) *The Rodale Book of Composting*. Emmaus, PA: Rodale Press, 1992. 278p
A comprehensive, readable book which gives history, benefits, techniques, materials, and machines related to composting. For those who want to know everything about composting.

Soil animals

Lavies, Bianca. *Compost Critters*. New York, NY: Dutton Children's Books, 1993. 32p
A superb collection of color photographs of the smaller denizens of a compost pile such as springtails, sowbugs, and mites. The text describes the sequence of events and creatures which gradually change organic garbage from weeds, leaves, fruit and vegetable leftovers into moist, dark, nutritious material perfect for plants.

Schaller, Friedrich. *Soil Animals*. Ann Arbor, MI: University of Michigan Press, 1968. 144p
If you were enticed by the chapter on "other critters," but are not yet ready for a zoology text, look at this well-illustrated little book describing collection methods, characteristics, importance, habits, and behavior of animals that live in the soil. It's out of print, so try your library.

Worm books for kids

Appelhof, Mary, Mary Frances Fenton and Barbara Loss Harris. *Worms Eat Our Garbage: Classroom Activities for a Better Environment*. Kalamazoo, MI: Flower Press, 1993. 232p
For teachers, parents, and the children with whom they work and play, this book presents over 150 exciting, educational, fun, and interesting activities using worms as their common denominator to teach math, science, language arts, and creativity. In use in thousands of classrooms in the United States and Australia, this popular book is gaining in popularity among the home-schooling movement.

Lauber, Patricia. *Earthworms, Underground Farmers*. New York, NY: Henry Holt, 1994. 55p
This informative book uses clear language, excellent black and white illustrations, and colorful photographs to teach youngsters about earthworms. A noted author of dozens of children's books talks about worm farms, earthworm body parts, how worms move, how they breathe, and how they make more worms. She emphasizes their role in recycling organic matter by decomposing plant litter and by serving as food for animals such as birds and moles.

Glaser, Linda. *Wonderful Worms*. Brookfield, CT: The Millbrook Press, 1992. 32p
Illustrations provide unusual perspectives for showing worms. A cross-section of soil shows feet walking on it, plants growing on top with roots underneath, or rocks nestled into the earth.

Henwood, Chris. *Keeping Minibeasts: Earthworms*. New York, NY: Franklin Watts, 1991. 30p
The outstanding color photographs of earthworms in this book geared for young children make it interesting for adults as well. The book guides a child in finding, collecting, and caring for one or more soil-dwelling earthworms.

Pigdon, Keith and Marilyn Woolley. *Earthworms.* Cleveland, OH: Modern Curriculum Press. 1989. 24p
Color illustrations and simple text present information about earthworms such as anatomical features; what they eat; where they live; how they breed, hatch, and grow up; what kind of dangers they meet; and common myths.

Plater, Inge. *How Earthworms Live; Earthworms and Their Food; How Earthworms Grow.* Bothell, WA: The Wright Group, 19201 - 120th Avenue NE, Bothell, WA 98011. 1995. *(Earthworms,* series of 3 books, level 3) 24p
Excellent color photographs combined with illustrations and cartoons cover different aspects in the lives of earthworms.

Ross, Michael Elsohn. *Wormology.* Minneapolis, MN: Carolrhoda Books, Inc., c/o The Lerner Group, 241 First Avenue N, Minneapolis, MN 55401. 1996. 48p
A charming book with much kid appeal. It supports and encourages learning by inquiry by garnering questions from kids in second through sixth grades and devising ways to get earthworms to answer their questions.

Periodicals

Worm Digest, 4 issues per year, edited by Steven Frankel. Box 544, Eugene, OR 97440-0544. Subscription rates: $12 United States; US $16 Canada and Mexico; US $20 other countries.
Worm Digest is a 32-page newspaper that promotes the use of worms and worm composting for organic-waste conversion and soil enrichment. This interesting, fact-filled publication reports on worm-worthy news worldwide and has readers in all 50 states, throughout Canada, and 15 other countries.

Appendix C:
A metric scenario

Seemingly simple arithmetic conversions of English measurement units used in the United States to metric equivalents are not straightforward. Use of conversion tables in popular dictionaries give solutions that do not agree with those from simple ratio equations, given three other known quantities. For example, in Webster's 7th edition, the "measurement" entry gives the equivalent of one acre as 4047 square meters. Its "metric" entry, however, gives equivalents for one hectare as 10,000 square meters and 2.47 acres. Using the metric entry data to solve arithmetically for the equivalent of one acre gives 4048.6 square meters, as follows:

$$\frac{10,000 \text{sq m}}{x} = \frac{2.47 \text{ acres}}{1.0 \text{ acre}} \quad \text{can be rewritten as}$$

2.47 (x) = 1 (10,000) = 4048.6 sq m where pairs of opposite top nominators and bottom denominators are cross-multiplied. Following multiplication, the unknown denominator x (above) stands alone (below) and can determined by division,

$$x = \frac{1\,(10,000)}{2.47} = \frac{10,000}{2.47} = 4048.6 \text{sq m}$$

The difference beween the table (4047) and the arithmetic solution (4048.6) is 1.7 square meters, an area not only bigger than the footspace of a breadbox, but bigger than that of a very large steamer trunk. When this difference is further magnified by adding the dimension of depth (that is, cubes rather than squares), major variation in calculations can easily occur. Expressed as a percentage, however, it is just four one-hundredths of a percent (0.04%).

Terminology has been inconsistent over time. Webster's 7th neither defines "tonne" nor uses it in its measurement tables. Webster's 9th and other more current dictionaries, however, define it as a metric ton (1.1 U.S. tons or 2204 pounds in one table, but as 2240 pounds in another). The U.S. ton is 2000 pounds and sometimes is called a short ton.

Taking the previous discussion into account, the following version of "How many worms in an acre?" provides approximate metric equivalents for measurements originally made in English units.

How many worms in a hectare?

One year I counted and weighed all the earthworms I could handsort from the top 18cm of a 30 x 30cm square dug from my garden's soil. I counted 62 worms of all sizes, and found at least two species. If I had had a hectare under cultivation and if this were, in fact, a representative sample, the total population would have exceeded 6.8 million worms per hectare!

These 62 worms weighed 57 grams. Extended to one hectare, this would give a total weight of 6113 kilograms, or over six metric tons of worms in the top 18 centimeters of one hectare (10,000 square meters) of soil!

How much do their castings weigh?

Earthworms of the soil-dwelling type eat soil in their search for organic nutrients. They mix the soil with organic materials and bacteria in their intestines, and excrete the mixed deposit as castings. The weight of these castings per worm per day could easily equal the weight of the worm. Let's estimate conservatively that the weight of castings deposited per day from one worm is one-eighth the worm's weight. The total weight of castings produced per hectare per day would be 764 kilograms. Think of the worm's activity in producing those castings and their value to plants.

To estimate annual casting production, let's assume that the worms are active only 150 days of the year, giving 112 metric tons of castings per hectare per year. (If you have ever tossed a ton of manure onto a pickup truck and off again, you can begin to appreciate the work worms do for you in your garden.) Charles Darwin's approach in 1881 to estimating castings production was to collect, dry, and weigh all castings from a square yard of grassland for a whole year. He recorded from three to 16 tons per acre of dry earth annually ejected by worms in the form of castings.

How do agricultural practices affect earthworms?

Some modern agricultural practices have not only reduced soil earthworm and microbial populations, but also the amounts of organic matter present in the soil. Less organic matter results in less food for worms. In addition, plowing and tilling not only kills worms directly, but exposes them to predators and drying conditions. Worm burrows provide a means for water to move deeper into the soil. Plowing destroys worm burrows, reducing the capacity of the soil to hold water and increasing the possibility of flooding during torrential rains.

Crop management practices which result in increased worm populations have also demonstrated higher crop yields. Such practices include less tillage, planting cover crops, and retaining stubble, all methods that retain moisture and provide food for the worms. An example reported by John Buckerfield from Australia showed substantial grape yield increases when straw mulch and composted yard trimmings were applied underneath the vines. The increase in crop yield correlated with increased earthworm populations. Other promising research showed that applying vermicomposted grape residue and cattle manure to vineyards and other horticultural crops increased yields. Applied under mulch, these applications also helped reduce the need for irrigation and weed control.

Apparently, many climatic regions could benefit from applying this knowledge related to earthworms, whether they be earthworkers or vermicomposters. Part of my work is to help people understand how earthworms enhance the quality of our soils, our food, and our lives. I also want to discourage those practices that kill these amazing creatures. Their production of natural manure has been creating and improving soils for millions of years.

Glossary

acid Normal product of decomposition. Redworms do best in a slightly acid (pH just less than 7) environment. Below pH5 can be toxic. Addition of pulverized egg shells and/or lime helps to neutralize acids in a worm bin. *See also* pH.

aggregation Clustering, as of soil particles, to form granules that aid in aeration and water penetration.

aeration Exposure of a medium to air to allow exchange of gases.

aerobic Pertaining to the presence of free oxygen. Organisms that utilize oxygen to carry out life functions.

albumin A protein in cocoons that serves as a food source for embryonic worms.

alkaline Containing bases (hydroxides, carbonates) which neutralize acids to form salts. *See also* pH.

anaerobic Pertaining to the absence of free oxygen. Organisms that can grow without oxygen present.

anaerobiosis Life in an environment without oxygen or air.

anterior Toward the front.

Ardox nails Nails with a spiral shape designed to increase holding power.

bedding Moisture-retaining medium used to house worms.

bedrun Worms of all sizes, as contrasted with selected breeders. Also pit-run, run-of-pit.

bio-degradable Capable of being broken down into simpler components by living organisms.

biological control Management of pests within reasonable limits by encouraging natural predator/prey relationships and avoiding use of toxic chemicals.

biomass That part of a given habitat consisting of living matter, expressed as weight of organisms per unit area. Recommended biomass of worms for vermicomposting is about one pound per square foot (one-half kilogram per one-tenth square meter) surface area of bedding.

breeders Sexually mature worms as identified by a clitellum.

buffer A substance which renders a system less sensitive to fluctuations between acidity and alkalinity. Humus serves as a buffer in soil.

calcium carbonate Used to reduce acidity in worm bins and agricultural soils. *See* lime.

castings *See* worm castings; vermicast.

CCA Term for wood treated with a preservative containing copper, chromium, and arsenic to control against termite and fungus damage. Also called pressure-treated wood. Because of its toxicity it should not be used for home interiors or cutting-boards or counter-tops. One should wear goggles and a dust mask when power-sawing (preferably outdoors), and wash exposed parts of the body before eating, drinking, or using tobacco. Work clothes should be washed separately from other household clothing. Disposal of unused wood could be a problem, since it should not be burned in a stove or fireplace. Treated wood from industrial sources should be burned only in approved commercial or industrial incinerators.

CDX plywood CD plywood has knotholes and small splits present, as contrasted with a higher, grade such as AB which has one side smooth and free from defects. Exterior (X) plywood is bonded with waterproof glue and suitable for use outside.

cellulose An inert compound containing carbon, hydrogen, and oxygen which is a component of worm beddings. Wood, cotton, hemp, and paper fibers are primarily cellulose.

chlorosis Abnormal yellowing of plant tissues caused by nutrient deficiency or activities of a pathogen.

clitellum A swollen region containing gland cells which secrete the cocoon material. Also called girdle or saddle.

cocoon Structure formed by the clitellum which houses embryonic worms until they hatch.

coir Coconut fiber or dust, a waste product of the coconut industry. Sold in compressed blocks as a worm bedding, it has high water-holding capacity. Used as substitute for peat moss.

compactor-transfer station A facility which accepts solid waste and compacts it prior to transfer to a landfill or other refuse disposal facility.

compost Biological reduction of organic waste to humus. Used to refer to both the process and the end product. One composts leaves, manure, and garden residues to obtain compost which enhances soil texture and fertility when used in gardens.

consumer An organism that feeds on other plants or animals.

culture To grow organisms under defined conditions. Also, the product of such activity, as a bacterial culture.

cyst A sac, usually spherical, surrounding an animal in a dormant state.

decomposer An organism that breaks down cells of dead plants and animals into simpler substances.

decomposition The process of breaking down complex materials into simpler substances. End products of much biological decomposition are carbon dioxide and water.

diatomaceous earth Finely pulverized shells of diatoms used for insect control.

earthworm A segmented worm of the Phylum Annelida, most of whose 4400 species are terrestrial.

egg A female sex cell capable of developing into an organism when fertilized by a sperm.

egg case *See* cocoon.

Eisenia andrei Scientific name for worm commonly used for vermicomposting. *Eisenia andrei* is a close relative of *Eisenia fetida*. It is entirely reddish, does not appear striped, and is sometimes known as the "red tiger" worm.

Eisenia fetida (formerly *Eisenia foetida*) Scientific name for the most common redworm used for vermicomposting. It is characterized by lack of pigment between its reddish segments, thus showing a striping pattern. Some common names include tiger worm, manure worm, and brandling.

enchytraeids Small, white, segmented worms common in vermicomposting systems.

enzyme Complex protein which provides a site for specific chemical reactions.

Eudrilus eugeniae Scientific name for large worm of tropical origin commonly known as the African nightcrawler. Not suitable for vermicomposting in cold climates.

excrete To separate and to discharge waste.

feces Waste discharged from the intestine through the anus. Manure.

fertilize To supply nutrients to plants or to impregnate an egg.

genus (pl. **genera**) A category of classification grouping organisms with a set of characteristics more generalized than species characteristics.

girdle *See* clitellum.

gizzard Region in anterior portion of digestive tract whose muscular contractions help grind food.

green business A business that prioritizes the environment in its practices and products. Typical policies include maximizing energy efficiency, avoiding pollution, and creating markets for recycled materials.

grit Coarse or fine abrasive particles used by worm in gizzard to grind food.

hatchlings Worms as they emerge from a cocoon.

heavy metals Dense metals such as cadmium, lead, copper, and zinc which can be toxic in small concentrations. Build up of heavy metals in garden soil should be avoided.

hemoglobin Iron-containing compound in blood responsible for its oxygen-carrying capacity.

hermaphrodite Term for an organism which possesses both male and female sex organs. Most earthworms are hermaphrodites (some are parthenogenetic, that is, have only female sex organs).

humus Complex, highly stable material formed during breakdown of organic matter.

hybrid Resulting from mating between individuals of two different species, normally producing sterile offspring, as when a horse-donkey breeding produces a mule. The term "hybrid redworm" is fairly common in the worm industry, but scientists do not accept this as proper usage of the term. No proof for hybridization among worm species exists.

hydrated lime Calcium hydroxide. Do not use in worm bins. *See also* lime.

inoculate To provide an initial set of organisms for a new culture.

leach To run water through a medium, causing soluble materials to dissolve and drain off.

leaf mold Leaves in an advanced stage of decomposition.

lime A calcium compound which helps reduce acidity in worm bins. Use calcium carbonate, ground limestone rock, egg shells, or oyster shells. Avoid caustic, slaked, and hydrated lime.

litter (leaf) Organic material on forest floor containing leaves, twigs, decaying plants, and associated organisms.

Lumbricus rubellus Scientific name for a worm species found in compost piles and soils rich in organic matter. Sometimes known as red marsh worm, dung worm, redworm.

Lumbricus terrestris Scientific name for large burrow-dwelling nightcrawler. Known commonly as Canadian nightcrawler in United States, dew worm in Canada.

microbes Very minute living things, whether plant or animal; bacteria, protozoa, fungi, actinomycetes.

macroorganism Organism large enough to see by naked eye.

microorganism Organism requiring magnification for observation.

monoculture Cultivation of a single species.

nematodes Small (usually microscopic) roundworms with both free-living and parasitic forms. Not all nematodes are pests.

nightcrawler A common name for *Lumbricus terrestris*, a large, burrow-inhabiting earthworm.

optimal Most favorable conditions, such as for growth or for reproduction.

organic Pertaining to or derived from living organisms.

overload To deposit more garbage in a worm bin than can be processed aerobically.

pasteurize To expose to heat long enough to destroy certain types of organisms.

pathogen Disease-producing organism.

peat moss Sphagnum moss which is mined from bogs, dried, ground, and used as an organic mulch. Although acidic, its light, fluffy texture and excellent moisture retention characteristics make it a good medium for shipping worms. No longer recommended as a worm bedding because it is a limited resource and suitable alternatives exist.

Perionyx excavatus Scientific name for a tropical worm species found in India, southern parts of the United States, Australia, and elsewhere. One common name is Indian blue worm. Not suitable for vermicomposting in cold climates.

perlite A lightweight volcanic glass used to increase aeration in potting mixtures.

pH An expression for degree of acidity and alkalinity based upon the hydrogen ion concentration. The pH scale ranges from 0 to 14; pH7 being neutral; less than 7, acid; greater than 7, alkaline.

pharynx Muscular region of the digestive tract immediately posterior to a worm's mouth.

pit-run *See* bedrun.

population density Number of specfic organisms per unit area, for example, 1000 worms per square foot.

posterior Toward the rear, back, or tail.

potting soil A medium for potting plants.

pot worms *See* enchytraeids.

prostomium Sensitive fleshy lobe protruding above the mouth.

protein Complex molecule containing carbon, hydrogen, oxygen, and nitrogen; a major constituent of meat. Worms are approximately 60% protein.

putrefaction Anaerobic decomposition of organic matter, especially protein, characterized by disagreeable odors.

redworm A common name for *Eisenia fetida, Eisenia andrei,* and also *Lumbricus rubellus*. *Eisenia fetida* and *Eisenia andrei* are the primary redworms used for vermicomposting.

regenerate To replace lost parts.

run-of-pit *See* bedrun.

saddle *See* clitellum.

salt Salts are formed in worm bins as acids and bases combine, having been released from decomposition of complex compounds.

secrete To release a substance that fulfills some function within the organism. Secretion of slime by a worm helps retain moisture and protect its body from injury by coarse soil particles.

segment One of numerous disc-shaped portions of an earthworm's body bounded anteriorly and posteriorly by membranes.

seminal fluid Fluid which contains sperm that are transferred to an earthworm's mate during copulation.

setae Bristles on each segment used in locomotion.

sexually mature Possessing a clitellum and capable of breeding.

side dressing Application of nutrients on soil surface away from stem of plants.

slaked lime Calcium hydroxide. Do not use in worm bins.

species Basic category of biological classification, characterized by individuals which can breed together and produce offspring which can also produce young.

sperm Male sex cells.

sperm-storage sacs Pouches which hold sperm received during mating.

subsoil Mineral-bearing soil located beneath humus-containing topsoil.

taxonomist A scientist who specializes in classifying and naming organisms.

top dressing Nutrient-containing materials placed on the soil surface around the base of plants.

toxic Poisonous, life-threatening.

toxoplasmosis Disease caused by the protozoan *Toxoplasma gondii*.

vermicast A single worm casting or a quantity of worm castings. Worms "work" material by ingesting, excreting, and re-ingesting it. Vermicast is extensively worm-worked and re-worked. It may be overworked and has probably lost plant nutrients as compared to vermicompost. Vermicast has a fine, smooth texture which may dry with a crust on the surface. *See also* worm casting.

vermicompost Mixture of partially decomposed organic waste, bedding, and worm castings. Contains recognizable fragments of plant, food, or bedding material, as well as cocoons, worms, and associated organisms. As a verb, to carry out composting with worms.

vermicomposting The process of using worms and associated organisms to break down organic waste into material containing nutrients for plant growth.

vermiculite Lightweight potting material produced through expansion of mica by means of heat.

vermiculture The raising of earthworms under controlled conditions.

white worms *See* enchytraeids.

worm bin Container designed to accommodate a vermicomposting system.

worm castings Undigested material, soil, and bacteria deposited through the anus. Worm manure. *See also* vermicast.

worm:garbage ratio When setting a worm bin, the relationship between weight of worms and weight of garbage to be processed on a daily basis.

Bibliography

Appelhof, Mary. "Basement worm bins produce potting soil and reduce garbage." Kalamazoo, MI: Flowerfield Enterprises, 1973. 2p

_____. "Composting your garbage with worms." Kalamazoo, MI: Kalamazoo Nature Center, 1981, 1979. 4p

_____. "Household scale vermicomposting," in *Workshop on the Role of Earthworms in the Stabilization of Organic Residues. Vol. I: Proceedings*, compiled by Mary Appelhof. Kalamazoo, MI: Beech Leaf Press, 1981. p232-240.

_____. "Vermicomposting on a household scale," in *Soil Biology as Related to Land Use Practices, Proceedings of the International Colloquium on Soil Zoology*, edited by Daniel Dindal. Washington, D.C.: U.S. EPA, 1980. p157-160

_____. *Videomicroscopy of Live Earthworms*, final report to National Science Foundation. Kalamazoo, MI: Flowerfield Enterprises, 1994. 27p (SBIR Award No. III-936127)

_____. *Winter Composting with Worms*, final report to National Center for Appropriate Technology. Kalamazoo, MI: Kalamazoo Nature Center, 1979. 13p

_____. "Worms—a safe, effective garbage disposal,"*Organic Gardening and Farming*, 21(8):1974; p65-69.

_____. "Worms vs. high technology," *Creative Woman*, 4(1): 1980; p23-28.

Appelhof, Mary, Katie Webster, and John Buckerfield. "Vermicomposting in Australia and New Zealand," *BioCycle*, 37:1996 June; p63-66.

Appelhof, Mary, Michael Tenenbaum, and Randy Mock. "Energy considerations: resource recycling and energy recovery," presentation before the Resource Recovery Advisory Committee, South Central Michigan Planning Council. Kalamazoo, MI, July 1980.

Appelhof, Mary, Michael Tenenbaum, Randy Mock, Cheryl Poche, and Scott Geller. *Biodegradable Solid Waste Conversion into Earthworm Castings*, final report to National Science Foundation. Kalamazoo, MI: Flowerfield Enterprises, 1981. 78p (ISP-8009755)

Ball, Ian R., and Ronald Slys. "Turbellaria: Tricladida: Terricola," in *Soil Biology Guide,* edited by Daniel L. Dindal. New York, NY: John Wiley and Sons, 1990. 1349p

Barrett, Thomas J. *Harnessing the Earthworm.* Boston, MA: Wedgwood Press, 1959, 1947. 166p

Bhawalkar, Uday S. *Vermiculture Ecotechnology.* Pune, India: Bhawalkar Earthworm Research Institute, 1995. 329p

Bogdanov, Peter. *Commercial Vermiculture: How to Build a Thriving Business in Redworms.* Merlin, OR: Vermico, 1996. 83p

Brown, Amy. *Earthworms in New Zealand.* Auckland: Reed Publishing, 1995. 110p

_____. *Earthworms Unlimited.* Maryborough, Victoria, Australia: Kangaroo Press Pty Ltd, 1994. 80p

Buckerfield, J.C., and K.A. Webster. "Earthworms, mulching, soil moisture and grape yields," *Australian and New Zealand Wine Industry Journal,* 11(1):1996. p47-53.

_____. "Earthworms as indicators of sustainable production," in *Proceedings Inaugural Ecological Economics Conference,* November 19-23. Coffs Harbour, New South Wales, 1995. p333-339.

Cooke, A. "The effects of fungi on food selection by *Lumbricus terrestris* L.," in *Earthworm Ecology,* edited by J.E. Satchell. Cambridge, England: Chapman and Hall, 1983. p365-373.

Cresswell, G.C. "Coir dust—a viable alternative to peat?" Rydalmere, New South Wales, Australia: Biological and Chemical Research Institute. WorldWideWeb, 1994. 7p

Darwin, Charles. *The Formation of Vegetable Mould, through the Action of Worms, with Observations on their Habits.* New York: D. Appleton and Company, 1898, 1881. 326p

Dindal, Daniel L. "Ecology of compost: a public involvement project." Syracuse, New York: NY State Council of Environmental Advisors and the State University of New York College of Environmental Science and Forestry, 1972. 12p

Edwards, C.A., and Edward F. Neuhauser, editors. *Earthworms in Waste and Environmental Management.* The Hague, Netherlands: SPB Academic Publishing BV, 1988. 392p

Edwards, C. A., and J. R Lofty. *Biology of Earthworms,* 2nd edition. London, United Kingdom: Chapman and Hall, 1977. 333p

Edwards, C.A., and P. J. Bohlen. *Biology and Ecology of Earthworms,* 3rd edition. London, United Kingdom: Chapman and Hall, 1996. 426p

Ernst, David. *The Farmer's Earthworm Handbook: Managing Your Underground Money-Makers.* Brookfield, WI: Lessiter Publications, 1995. 112p

Geller, E. Scott, Richard A. Winett, and Peter B. Everett. *Preserving the Environment.* Elmsford, NY: Pergamon, 1982. 338p

Goldstein, Jerome. *Recycling.* New York, NY: Schocken Books, 1979. 238p

Goldstein, Nora. "The state of garbage in America,"*BioCycle,* 38:1997; p62-67.

Hambly, Sam. "The Allsaw insulated composter." Downsview, Ontario: Camp Allsaw, date unknown. 3p

Handreck, Kevin Arthur. "Earthworms for gardeners and fishermen." Adelaide, Australia: CSIRO Division of Soils, 1978. 15p

Hartenstein, R., E.F. Neuhauser, and J. Collier. "Accumulation of heavy metals in the earthworm *Eisenia foetida,*" *Journal of Environmental Quality,* 9:1980; p23-26.

Hartenstein, R., E.F. Neuhauser, and D.L. Kaplan. "Reproductive potential of the earthworm *Eisenia foetida,*" *Oecologia,* 43:1979; p329-340.

Hendrix, Paul, editor. *Earthworm Ecology and Biogeography in North America.* Boca Raton, FL: Lewis Publishers, 1995. 244p

Home, Farm and Garden Research Associates. *Let an Earthworm Be Your Garbage Man.* Eagle River, WI: Shields, 1954. 46p

Institute for Local Self-Reliance. Three discussion papers of the Grassroots Recycling Network. WorldWideWeb, 1997. 13p

James, Sam. Personal communication. Fairfield, IA: Maharishi University, 1997 March 10.

Kaplan, D.L., R. Hartenstein, and E.F. Neuhauser. "Coprophagic relations among the earthworms *Eisenia foetida, Eudrilus eugeniae* and *Amynthas* spp," *Pedobiologia,* 20:1980; p74-84.

Kaplan, D.L., E.F. Neuhauser, R. Hartenstein, and M.R. Malecki. "Physicochemical requirements in the environment of the earthworm *Eisenia foetida,*" *Soil Biology and Biochemistry*, 12(1):1980; p347-352.

Kretzschmar, A., editor. *ISEE 4: 4th International Symposium on Earthworm Ecology*. Special Issue of *Soil Biology Biochemistry*, 24(12): 1992. 333p

Martin, Deborah L. , and Grace Gershuny, editors. *The Rodale Book of Composting*. Emmaus, PA: Rodale Press, 1992. 278p

Martin, J.P., J.H. Black, and R.M. Hawthorne. "Earthworm biology and production." University of California Cooperative Extension, 1976. 10p (Leaflet #2828)

McCormack, Jeffrey H. "A review of whitefly traps," *The IPM Practitioner*, 3(10):1981; p3.

Minnich, Jerry, and Marjorie Hunt. *The Rodale Guide to Composting*. Emmaus, PA: Rodale Press, 1979. 405p

Mitchell, Myron J., Robert M. Mulligan, Roy Hartenstein, and Edward F. Neuhauser. "Conversion of sludges into 'topsoils' by earthworms," *Compost Science*: 1977 Jul/Aug; p28-32.

Morgan, Charlie. *Earthworm Feeds and Feeding*, 6th edition. Eagle River, WI: Shields, 1972. 90p

Munday, Vivian, and J. Benton Jones, Jr. "Worm castings: how good are they as a potting medium?" *Southern Florist and Nursery-man*, 94(2):1981; p21-23.

Neuhauser, E.F., D.L. Kaplan, M.R. Malecki, and R. Hartenstein. "Materials supporting weight gain by the earthworm *Eisenia foetida* in waste conversion systems," *Agricultural Wastes*, 2:1980; p43-60.

Neuhauser, E.F., R. Hartenstein, and D.L. Kaplan. "Second progress report on potential use of earthworms in sludge management," in *Proceedings of Eighth National Conference on Sludge Composting*. Silver Springs, MD: Information Transfer, Inc., 1979. p238-241.

Myers, Ruth. A *Worming We Did Go!* Elgin, IL: Shields, 1968. 71p

Rao, B. R., I. Karuna Sagar, and J.V. Bhat. "*Enterobacter aerogenes* infection of *Hoplochaetella suctoria*," in *Earthworm Ecology*, edited by J.E. Satchell. Cambridge, England: Chapman and Hall, 1983. p383-393.

Reinecke, A.J., S.A. Viljoen, and R.J. Saayman. "The suitability of *Eudrilus eugeniae, Perionyx excavatus* and *Eisenia fetida* (Oligochaeta) for vermicomposting in southern Africa in terms of their temperature requirements." *Soil Biology Biochemistry,* 24: 1992; p1295-1307.

Reynolds, John W. *The Earthworms (Lumbricidae and Sparganophilidae) of Ontario.* Toronto, Canada: Royal Ontario Museum, 1977. 141p

Rouelle. J. "Introduction of amoebae and *Rhizobium japonicum* into the gut of *Eisenia fetida* (Sav.) and *Lumbricus terrestris* L.," in *Earthworm Ecology,* edited by J.E. Satchell. Cambridge, England: Chapman and Hall, 1983. p375-381.

Satchell, John E. "Earthworm microbiology," in *Earthworm Ecology: From Darwin to Vermiculture,* edited by J.E. Satchell. Cambridge, England: Chapman and Hall, 1983. p351-364.

_____. "Earthworm evolution: Pangaea to production prototype," in *Workshop on the Role of Earthworms in the Stabilization of Organic Residues. Vol. I: Proceedings,* compiled by Mary Appelhof. Kalamazoo, MI: Beech Leaf Press, 1981. p3-35.

_____. "Lumbricidae," in *Soil Biology,* edited by A. Burges and F. Raw. London and New York: Academic Press, 1967. p259-322.

Schaller, Friedrich. *Soil Animals.* Ann Arbor, MI: University of Michigan Press, 1968. 144p

Seldman, Neil N. "Recycling—history in the United States," in *Encyclopedia of Energy Technology and the Environment,* 1995. p2352-2368.

Vick, Nicholas A. "Toxoplasmosis," in *Grinker's Neurology,* 7th edition. Springfield, IL: Charles C. Thomas Publishers, 1976.

White, Stephen. "A vermi-adventure to India!," *Worm Digest,* 15:1997; p1,27,30.

Worden, Diane D., editor. *Workshop on the Role of Earthworms in the Stabilization of Organic Residues, Vol. II Bibliography.* Kalamazoo, MI: Beech Leaf Press, 1981. 492p

INDEX

Index entries refer to subjects in the Foreword, Chapters 1-14, Afterword, and Appendix B. *Italic page numbers* refer to figures.

Acarina. *See* mites
acidity, 1–2, 4, 34–35, 37, 40, 108, 111
actinomycetes, 96–*97*
aeration, 4, 9–10, 92
   bin holes, 1, *18*–19, 23, 28–29, 70
   mesh openings, 12–13, 26
   need for, 5, 12–13, 16, 71
   soffit vents, 12, *20*, 24, *28*
aerobic conditions, 13, 34–35, 68, 70, 103
aesthetics, 5, 10, 20, 24–25, 65, 67
African nightcrawlers, 41
African violets, *114*–115
air, 1, 4, 12–13, 34, 89, 92
   circulation of, 5, 24, 28, 30
alkalinity, 4, 111, 114, 116
ammonia, 37, 67
anaerobiosis, 2, 13, 30, 68, 71
andrei, E., 40–41
angle worms, 42–43
ants, 65, 95–*97, 107*
Aporrectodea trapezoides, 43
Aporrectodea tuberculata, 43
Aporrectodea turgida, 43
Appelhof, Mary, books, 133, 137
apple pomace worms, 38
aromatic materials, 25–26, 93. *See also* smells
arsenic, 16, 107
attitudes, toward
   bins, x, 75–76, 90, 108
   wastes, 14, 62, 120, 123
attractiveness. *See* aesthetics
Australia, 26–28, 99, 120, 129
avocado pits, germinating, 119

bacteria, 2, 35, 68, 70, 76, 91, 96–*97, 109*–111
bait worms. *See* fish bait
band, worm. *See* clitellum
banded breeders, 45

barium, in colored ink, 32
Barrett, Thomas, 134
basements, worm bins in, x, 3, 10, 86–88
beddings, worm, 26, 30–37, 46
   additions to, 35–37, 92
   air and, 12–13, 30, 76, 92
   cautions about, 32–36
   decomposition of, 5, 30–31, 78, 110
   as food, 7, 30, 32–33, 50
   kinds of, 27, *28,* 31–35, 99
   moisture and, 2, 4, 15, 31–35, 58–59, 61, 73, 76
   preparation of, 56–59, 82
   as shipping media, 35, 59–60
   system maintenance and, 1, 6, 8, 31, 50, 60–61, 69, 77–78, *81, 83–84, 86*
   temperature of, 4, 33, 42, 75
bedrun worms, 54
beetle mites, *97, 101, 109*
beetles, 95–*97,* 101, 103
benches, as bins, *11, 19, 20–25*
biomass, 51, 54, 110, 128–129
Bisesi, Michael, 75–76
body fluids, worm, 46, 58, 60, 96
   secretions, 92, 100, 112
body systems, worm
   circulatory, 46, 48
   digestive, 5, 13, 35, 49, 70–71, 91, *91*–92, 100, 108
   excretory, 4, 5, 50, 76, 92, 128–129
   locomotive, 13–14, 18, 30, 41, 43
   muscular, 43, 91, *91,* 93
   respiratory, 4–5, 92
   sensory, 90
   sexual, 40–41, 45–52, *47,* 74
Bogdanov, Peter, 135
bones, as wastes, 64–67
brandling worms, 38

breeder worms, 45, 48–49, 51, 54
bristles, worm (setae), 43
Brown, Amy, 131, 133–134
Brown, Mary, xi
Buckerfield, John, 129
burrows, 38, 42–43, 91, 129
burying garbage in worm bins,
    13–15, 42, 60–67, 69–73
  coverings needed for, 61, 66, 84,
    102–103
  difficulties of, 31, 33, 71
  as system maintenance, 1–2, 7,
    60–61, 77–78, 83–84
  techniques, 60–61, 70–72
  types of waste, 6, 62–67
  worm:garbage ratio, x, 52–53

cadmium, in colored ink, 32
calcium, as nutrient, 111, 114
calcium carbonate, 36, 64, 92
California, x, 26
Canada, 27, 35, 43, 85, 87–88
Can-O-Worms™, 26–27, 85
capsules, egg. See cocoons
carabids. See beetles
carbon, 30, 66, 69, 76, 95, 120, 122
carbon dioxide, 5, 13, 75, 92, 99,
    114
castings. See worm castings
castings tea. See vermicompost
    tea
catchment trays, 26–27, 75–76
CDX plywood, 17–20, 25
centipedes, 33, 95, 97, 99
chemical salts, 114–116
chicken bones, 65–66
chlorosis, 115
chromium, uses of, 16, 32
citrus waste, 62–64, 70
clitellum, 43, 45–47, 74
coconut fiber, 27, 33–34
cocoons, 2, 5, 46–49, 47, 54, 69, 74,
    83, 110, 112
coir. See coconut fiber
Collembola, 97, 98
color, ink, 32
colors, worm, 38–39, 41, 43

compaction, bedding, 13, 31, 33
competition, 49–50, 98, 100
composting, 97, 135–136
  indoors, ix–x
  outdoors, ix, 4, 7, 79, 108
  with worms. See vermicom-
    posting
control measures, for
  moisture, 4, 23, 25, 75–77, 82
  pests, 12, 24, 65, 69, 101–107,
    111, 117
  salts, 114–116, 118–119
  smells, 13, 30, 37, 64, 71–72,
    102–103
  temperature, 4, 10, 86–89
  worm populations, 49–50, 78,
    100, 113, 129
copper, in preservatives, 15–16
crop management, 129, 131–132

dairy wastes, 65, 67
Darwin, Charles, 128–129
deaths, causes of worm, 4–5
  castings and, 7, 50
  chemicals, 16, 33, 36, 67, 93
  predation, 94, 99–100, 129
  smothering, 13, 16, 60
  starvation, 49–50, 54, 129
  temperature extremes, 3, 41–42,
    59, 89
decomposers, 69, 95–109
  dead worms and, 5–6, 50, 89, 93
  food web of, 96–97, 98
  microorganisms as, 2, 13, 49, 65,
    75
DeMott, Jean, 77
Dendrobaena octaedra, 43
Dendrodrilus rubidus, 43
dew worms, 42–43
Dindal, Dan, 66, 95–97, 135–136
diseases, human, 37, 67–68, 107–
    108
diseases, plant, 111, 115
diversity, biological. See under
    species (biological)
drainage techniques, bin, 26–27,
    29, 75–77

Drosophila, 102, 104
dung worms, 38, 40–41

earthworkers. *See* earthworms, soil-dwelling species
earthworm mites, 101
earthworms, 90, 96–98, 126, 129, 131–135, 137–138
  common names for, 38–39, 42
  composting with, ix, 4, 38, 110
  research, 42–43, 129, 132–133
  sex of, 45, *47*
  soil-dwelling species, 38, *40*–43, 100, 111–112, 128–129
  weight. *See* biomass
ecosystems, 96–*97,* 108–109, 127
  recycling in, xii, 120
Edwards, Clive, 115–116, 132–133
Edwards, Roy, 132
egg cases, worm. *See* cocoons
egg shells, 15, 36, 62–64, 70, *97*
Eggan, Al, 26
Eisenia andrei, 40–41
Eisenia fetida, 39–41, 40–41, 94, 112
enchytraeids, 96–*97, 98, 109,* 117
Enemark, Gail, *10*
energy flow, xi, *97,* 120–122
England, 38, 115–116
environmental factors, and
  citizens as consumers, xi–xii, 15–16, 37, 122–124, 126–127
  pest control, 106, 111
  worm bins, 1, 3–7, 10, 12, 34–35, 71, 78, 88–89
  worm biology, 48–50, 78, 94, 129
enzymes, 92, 100, 110
Ernst, David, 131–132
Eudrilus eugeniae, 41
eugeniae, E., 41
Europe, 42, 100, 115–116
evaporation, 4, 82, 89
excavatus, P., 41

fecal worms, 38
feces. *See* manures, animal

fertilizers, x, 66–67, 111, 114, 126–127. *See also* vermicompost
fetida, E., 39–41, 94, 112
fibers, 25, 27, 30, 32–34
fines, powdered. *See* rock dust
finishes, wood, 16, 20, *20*–21
fish bait, worms as, x, 5–6, 38, 44–45, 51, 78, 126–127
flatworms, *97,* 100
flies, 12, 65, 69, 96–*97,* 102–107, 121
Flowerfield Enterprises, 28
foetida, E., 39–41, 94, 112
food webs, in compost, 96–*97*
formicids. *See* ants
Frankel, Steven, 138
fruit flies, 10, 102–107
fungi, 2, 35, 70, 91, 108, 111. *See also* molds

garbage. *See* organic wastes
Gardener's Supply, 26
gardens, 41, 43, 128
  castings for, 78, 117–119
  meat waste burial in, 66–67
  vermicompost in, x, 5, 8, 65, *81, 83, 86,* 110–111, *112–113,* 126
Geller, E. Scott, xi
genus names, system for, 39
girdle, worm. *See* clitellum
gizzards, worm, 35, *91*–92
glaciers, and worms, 36, 43
Glaser, Linda, 137
glass waste, x, 67, 122–125
gnats, 102
Grassroots Recycling Network, 121
grit, 35–37, *91*–92
growth inhibitors, plant
  salts as, 114–116, 119
grubs. *See* insects, larvae
gut, worm, 92, 108

habitats, worm, 33, 35, 39–41, 43, 55, 73, *97,* 112
Hagens, Bethe, xi

Hambly, Sam, *87*–88
handling worms. *See under*
      worms, segmented, care of
Hartenstein, Roy, 49
harvest techniques, 79–86
   alternate containers, 83
   divide and dump, 85–*86*
   dump and hand sort, 79–83,
      80–81
   worm self-sort, 83–85, *84*
harvests, kinds of
   vermicompost, 6, 8, 9, 34, *81*,
      82–83, *84*, 85–*86*
   worm, 2, 5–8, 9, 31, 78–86, *80–
      81, 84, 86*
   worm casting, 1, 6, 8, 27, 66, *80*,
      85, 117
hatchlings, 46–49, 69, 83, 96
heads, worm, 91, 93
heavy metals, 15–16, 32, 107, 126.
      See also metal names
hemoglobin, worm, 46, 96
Henderson, Hazel, xi
Henwood, Chris, 137
Holcombe, Dan, 134–135
home systems. *See* vermicompost-
      ing, home systems for
Hopp, Henry, 132
house plants, care of
   vermicompost for, 8, 9, 50, *81*,
      110, 126
   vermicompost tea for, 76–77
   worm castings for, 6, 78, *114–
      118*
humus, ix, 98, 111

identifying worms, 43
India, vermicomposting in, 66
Indian blue worm, 41
industrial waste, 120, 124
   reuse of, 34, 37
inks, toxicity of, 31–32
insects. *See also insect names*
   control of, 12, 24, 103–107
   larvae, 33, 103–106
   pupae, 103–104, 106

insulation, 9, 59–60, *87–88*
interdependent communities. *See*
      ecosystems
international interests
   in vermicomposting, xi, 26–27,
      66, *87–88*, 115–116, 129
   in Zero Waste, 120–121
iron, as nutrient, 111
isopods, *97,* 99

Kalamazoo Nature Center,
      projects, *63–65*, 115
kitchens, ix, 8–9, 86

ladybugs, 106
land snails, 97
landfills, 28, 123, 126
   recycling vs, xi, 121
Lauber, Patricia, 137
Lavies, Bianca, 136
lazy person's technique. *See*
      maintenance procedures,
      vermicomposting, low-
      level
lead, in colored ink, 32
leaf mold, 32–33, 99, 117
leaves, ix, 32–33, 43, *97*
life expectancy, 126
   materials, 16, 20, 25
   worms, 36, 49, 94, 111
light, reaction to, 48, 60–61, *79–80,*
      87, 90, 104
lime, hydrated, 36
limestone, powdered. *See* calcium
      carbonate
limonene, 64
litter boxes, 67–68, 107
litter (decaying vegetation), 35,
      40, 95, *97–98*
locations, worm bin, 3–5, 11
   cautions about, 4, 108
   indoors, 3, 8, 10, 42, 71–72, 86–
      87
   outdoors, 9, 67, 87–89
louvered vents, 12, *20,* 24, *28*
lumber, 34–35
   construction grades, *20*

lumber *(Continued)*
   framing lumber, 22–23, 24
   plywood, 16, *17–22*, 23, 25, *87–88*
   pressure-treated, 15–16
   scrap, 17, 122
Lumbricus rubellus, 40–41, 43
Lumbricus terrestris, 42–43, 94

maggots. *See* insects, larvae
magnesium, as nutrient, 116
maintenance procedures, vermicomposting, 1–2, 9, 13, 60, 77–79, 86
   high-level, 6, 78–79
   low-level, 7, 66–67, 78, 110, 113
   medium-level, 8, 79
manure worms, 38
manures, animal, 129. *See also* worm castings
   as beddings, 33, 59, 99
   as disease carriers, 67–68, 107–108
   as worm food, 115–116
manures, non-animal, ix, 4, 33, 40–41, 55, 129
Martin, Deborah L., 136
mating, 45–47, 74
matting problems, 13, 31, 33
meat scraps, 64–67, 95
metals, x, 67, 121–124. *See also* heavy metals
Michigan, 28–29, *63–64*, 77, 115
microorganisms, 60, 117
   as decomposers, ix, 13, 37, 49, 65, 70, 75, 113
   in soil, 111, 129
   as worm food, 2, 66, 96–98
millipedes, 95, *97*, 99–*100, 109*
minerals, 35–37, 91–92, 106
mites, 33, 96–*97*, 100–102, *109*, 117
moisture, 1, 4, 9, 13, 16, 89, 111. *See also* water
   beddings and, 4, 15, 29, 31–35, 58–61, 76, 83
   control, 23, 25–29, 75–77, 82. *See also* aeration

moisture *(Continued)*
   temperature extremes and, 59–60, 89
   in worm castings, 113–114
mold mites, *97, 101, 109*
molds, 2, 76, 96–*97*, 108–*109*
mucus, worm, 46–47, 112

naming worms, 38–39, 44
National Center for Appropriate Technology, projects, *63–65*
Nelson, Cindy, x
nematodes, *97*–98, 105–106, 111
New York, worm workers in, 66
New Zealand, 26, 42, 85, 100
newspaper waste, x, 32, 123–124
   as bin coverings, 73, 87
   as garbage wrap, 61, 69
   as shredded bedding, 28, 31–32, 56–59, 76, 95
newsprint. *See* inks; newspaper waste
nightcrawlers, 41–43, 132
   behaviors of, 46, 90–91
nitrogen, 66–67, 112, 114, 120
North America, worms in, 42–43
Northern Ireland, worms in, 100
nutrients, animal, 66
nutrients, plant, 13, 37. *See also* fertilizers
   in vermicompost, x, 50, 66, 110–111, *112–113*
   in vermicompost tea, 75–78
   in worm castings, 7, 114–116

oat products, as worm food, 60, 83
octaedra, D., 43
Octolasion tyrteum, 43
odors. *See* smells
Ohio, worm workers in, 115–116
1-2-3 worm box, 16–*18*, 57
orchard worms, 42–43
organic wastes
   accumulation, 4, 7, 14, 52–53, 89, 103
   decomposition, 5, 13, 49, 78, 82, 89, 95–103, 108–111

organic wastes (*Continued*)
handling procedures, 61, 65–72, 102–104, 121, 125–126
kinds of, 14–15, 62–67, 93, 115–116
landfills and, xii, 28, 126
recycling. *See* composting; vermicomposting
weighing, 52–53, 75
The Original Vermicomposter, 26
oxygen, 4, 13, 46, 76
need for, 5, 12, 60, 89, 92

packaging waste, x, 122–123, 125
paper. *See* newspaper waste
paper industry, 123–124
pasteurization, 117
pathogens, 67–68, 107–108, 111
patio bench worm bin, 9, *19–25, 57*, 67, 88
peat moss, 77, 115, 117
as bedding, 34–35, 70
Pennsylvania, 106
Perionyx excavatus, 41
perlite, 115, 117
pest control, 12, 24, 65–66, 69, 95, 102–107, 111, 117
pests, 33
pet feces, 67–68, 107
pH, 4, 34, 37, 39–40, 114, 116
phosphorus, as nutrient, 67, 111, 114
Pigdon, Keith, 138
pigmentation, 38–39, 41, 43
pill bugs, 99, *109*
pit-run worms, 54
planarians, *97*, 100–101
plants. *See also* house plants; nutrients, plant
fragments of, 5, 110–111
transplants, *112*, 118–119
plastic bins, 1, 26–29
moisture in, 4, 16, 28, 58, 75–77, 82
plastic sheets, uses of
bin coverings, 61, 73, 83–*84*
during harvests, 79–*81*

plastic sheets (Continued)
insulation, *87–88*
solar heating, *116*–117
plastic waste, 28–29, 67, 122, 125
Plater, Inge, 138
Plater, K. P., 106
plywood, *17–23*, 25, *87–88*
pot worms, 96–*97*, 98, *109*
potassium, as nutrient, 67, 111
potting soil, 7, 9, 77, *114*–118
predation and predators, 94, 96, 99–101, 129
preservatives, wood, 15–16, 20
prostomium, 43, *91*
protein waste, 64–67
protozoa, 2, 35, 67–68, 70, 91, 96–*97*
pupae. *See under* insects
putrefaction, 64, 71

rain worms, 42–43
record-keeping, 69, 74–75
recycled products, 16, 28, 122–124
recycling, xi, 121–124
garbage. *See* composting; vermicomposting
glass, 123–125
metal, 121–124
nature, 95–*97, 109*, 120, 126
paper, x, 32, 123–124
plastic, 28, 122, 125
red light, 90
red mites, 102
reducing consumption, 122
redworms. *See also Eisenia andrei; Eisenia fetida; Lumbricus rubellus*
acidity and, 4, 39–40
behavior, 13–14, 46, 74, 98, *109*
common names, 38–41
in nature, 35, 55, 112
oxygen needs, 12, 89
reproduction, 40, 45–52, 54, 96
temperatures for, 3–4, 33, 40, 87
vermicomposting with, ix–x, 33, *109*, 135
regeneration, body parts, 93

RELN Worm Factory (bin), 26–28
reproduction, worm, 45–52, 129
    eggs for, 45–48
    population controls on, 49–50,
        78, 100, 113, 129
    rate of, 38, 40–41, 45, 48–51, 54
    sperm for, 45–47
reusing wastes, 29, 34–36, 122–123
rock dust, 36–37, 92, 106
rodents, control of, 24, 65–66
roly-polies. *See* pill bugs
Ross, Michael E., 138
rotifers, 96–97
roundworms, *97–98*
rubellus, L., 40–41, 43
rubidus, D., 43
run-of-pit worms, 54

saddle, worm. *See* clitellum
sand, 37, 91, 117
Schaller, Friedrich, 136
science education, 43, 49, 64, 74,
        137–138
Seattle Tilth, 19
secretions, 46, 92, 100, 112
seed beds, 111–*112,* 118
seminal fluid, worm, 46
setae (bristles, worm), 43
Shields Earl B., 134
shredded paper, 31–32. *See also*
    under newspaper waste
slaked lime, 36
slaters, 99
slugs, *97*
smart-person's technique. *See*
        maintenance procedures,
        vermicomposting, low-
        level
smells, 30–35, 64–67, 102–*105*
    absence of, 13, 31–32, 34–35, 68,
        70
    control of, 13, 30, 37, 64, 71,
        102–103
    earthy, ix, 66, 82, 113–114
    objectionable, ix, 10, 13, 16, 33,
        39, 60, 64–67, 74, 121
snails, 95, *97*

snow fleas, 98
soffit vents, 12, *20, 24, 28*
soil, organisms in, 98, 136. *See also*
        earthworms, soil-dwelling
        species
soil blocks, homemade, 118
soils, 35, 128–129
    aeration, 43, 115, 117, 129
    mixed, 9, *40,* 43, 77, 114–118
    organic, *40*–41, 108, 111
    potting, 7, 9, 77, *114*–118
    topsoil, 92, 117, 128
sowbugs, 33, 70, 96–*97, 99, 109*
species (biological), 40–43
    diversity of, 45–46, 98, 101, 108,
        128
    names, 39, 42. *See also individual
        names*
sphagnum moss. *See* peat moss
spigots, drainage, 27, 29, 77
springtails, 70, 96–98, 100, *109,*
        117
Sri Lanka, 34
stink worms, 38
striped worms, 38
structural materials, bin, 15–26,
        28–29
Styrofoam®, *87*–88, 125
sulfur, as nutrient, 111
surface areas, and bins, 13–15
    worm:garbage ratio, 14, 53

tails, worm, 91, 93
Tasmania, 35
temperature, 1, 33, 39–42
    cocoons and, 2, 46, 48
    extremes, 3–4, 9, 10, 29, 55, 60,
        86–89, 117
terrestris, L., 42–43, 94
"The Three R's," 122–125
tiger worms, 39
top dressings, 112–*113,* 118
topsoil, 92, 113, 117, 128, 129
toxic substances, 36, 64, 102. *See
        also* heavy metals
    potential, 26, 31–32
    worm excretions as, 7, 49–50,
        67, 78

toxoplasmosis, 67–68, 68, 107
transplants. *See under* plants
trapezoides, A., 43
traps, 104–*105*, 106–107
trash, xii, 6, 28, 67, 125, 127
traveling worms, 13–14, 18, 30, 41
tuberculata, A., 43
turbellarians, *97*, 100
turgida, A., 43
2x2 worm bin, 18–19, 53, *57*, 79
tyrteum, O., 43

United States. *See also state names*
    economy of, xi, 122–124, 126
    recycling in, 121, 123
    regulations, 32, 65, 123
    vermicomposting in, xi, 19, 26–
        29
    worms in, 43, 100
unwanted organisms. *See* pests

vegetarian scraps, 14–15, 62–64,
    70–72, 74
vegetation, decaying. *See* litter
    (decaying vegetation)
ventilation. *See* aeration
vermicast, 5, 27, 30, 110
vermicompost, 5–6, 8–9, 67
    composition, 31, 37, 66, 82–83,
        108, 110–112, 117, 119
    harvesting, 34, *81*, 82–*86*
    production, 66, 70, 78
    uses, x, 66, 82–83, 111–*113*
vermicompost tea, 27, 75–77
vermicomposting, ix, 5
    convenience, 8–10, 68
    equipment, tools, and supplies,
        12–29, 37, 74–77, 79, 87–
        88
    expectations, xii, 6–8, 52, 126–
        127
    home systems for, 1–2, 5–11,
        14–15, 35, 62–72. *See also*
        worm bins
    international interest in, xi, 26–
        27, 66, *87*–88, 115–116,
        129

vermicomposting (*continued*)
    learning about, x, 2, 19, 26, 67,
        73–74, 109, 121
    organic wastes, 3, 5, 14–15, 34,
        43, 49, 88, 95, *97*, 115–
        116, 125–126
    outdoors, 9, 66, 87–89
    process, x, 27, 35, 95, 108
    worms for, 38–41, 44–45, 82, 85,
        126. *See also* redworms
vermiculite, 117
vermiculture, xii, 38, 133–135
    commercial, 35, 40–41, 50–51,
        54–55, 60, 87, 100–101
    harvests after, 2, 5–8, 78–86
    species competition in, 49–50,
        98, 100
Vermont, bins from, 26
vinegar flies, 102, 104

warnings about worm bins
    allergies, 108
    beddings, 32, 36
    locations, 4, 108
    materials, 15–16, 25–26, 58
    pests, 65, 102
    predators, 100–101
    wastes to avoid, 65, 67–68, 107–
        108
wastes
    garbage. *See* organic wastes
    natural, ix, 32–34, 36–37, 43, *97*
    recycling, x–xii, 16, 32, 121,
        123–125
    reducing, 122
    reusing, xi, 29, 34–35, 122–123
    Zero Waste and, 120–121
water, 13, 16, 92, 118, 120, 122. *See
    also* moisture
    as body fluid, 58, 60
    excess, problem-solving, 26–27,
        29, 75–77, 82
    retention, 43, 61, 73, 115, 117,
        129
water:bedding ratio, 58
white worms, 96–98, *109*, 117
winter composting, ix, 4, 7, 78,
    86–89

wood. *See* lumber
wooden bins, 1, 15–26, *87–88*
  cautions about, 15–16, 25–26
  family-sized, 16–25
    1-2-3 worm box, 16–*18, 57*
    patio bench, 19–25, *57*
    2x2 worm bin, 18–19, 53, *57*
woodlice, 99
worm bins, 1–2, 5, 12–29. *See also*
    plastic bins; vermicom-
    posting, home systems for;
    wooden bins
  cautions about. *See* warnings
    about worm bins
  commercial, 13, 16, 26–29, 37,
    85
  construction, 15–26, 28–29
  coverings, *19, 21–22,* 24, *25, 28,*
    61, 73, *87–88,* 106
  demonstrations with, x, 19, 28,
    63–65
  design, 16, 19, 29, 87–88
  as furniture, *10, 11, 19, 25*
  garbage for. *See* burying
    garbage in worm bins
  insulating, 9, *87–88*
  locations, 3–4, 8–11, 67, 86–89,
    108
  number, 7, 16, 71–72, 85, 88
  overloading, 71–72
  setting up, 7–8, 33, 44, 56–61
  shape, 12–*14,* 16, *18–19, 23, 25,*
    26, *27–28*
  size, 14–19, *23,* 26, 28, 52–53,
    56–*57*
  weight, 28, 35
  Zero Waste and, 121, 125–127
worm castings, 5–8, 113–119
  composition, 110, 113–116, 119
  harvesting of, 1, 6, 8, 27, 66, *80,*
    85, 117
  production, 5, 7, 14, 30–32, 43,
    49–50, 70, 77–78, 92, 110,
    128–129
  sterilizing, 116–117
  toxicity of, 7, 31, 49–50, 78
  weight, 128–129

worm growers. *See* vermiculture,
    commercial
Worm Summit (conference), x
worm workers, people as, 127
  activities of, x–xi, 73–74, 79, 84–
    85, 115–116
  learning from, x, 26, 66, 77, 87–
    88, 106, 129
Worm-a-way® 28–29, *57*
worm:garbage ratio, x, 52–53
worms. *See* flatworms; round-
    worms; worms, segmented
worms, segmented, x, 90, 94. *See*
    also body systems, worm
  books about, 131–135, 137–138
  buying, 7, 26, 40, 44, 54–55
  care of, x, 3–5, 7, 40–41, 49, 60,
    73–78, 82–83, 86–89
  in distress, 42, 71, 93
  food consumption by, 5, 13, 27,
    69–70, 91, 115–116
  health, 6–8, 13, 31, 78, 89
  kinds of, 27, 38–44. *See also*
    earthworms;
    enchytraeids; redworms
  maturity, 45, 48–49, 51, 54
  organisms associated with, 1–2,
    6, 33, 49–50, 60, 65, 69,
    95–109
  as products. *See* vermiculture
  roles of, 43, 70, 87
  shipping of, 35, 55, 59–60
  weight, x, 48, 51–54, 128–129
Worms Eat My Garbage (1982), xi–
    xii

yard wastes, ix, 4, 88, 129

zeolite, as bedding, 37
Zero Waste
  achieving, 122–125
  programs for, 120–121
  worm bins and, 121, 125–127

About the author

Mary Appelhof

With master's degrees in education and the biological sciences, Mary Appelhof founded Flowerfield Enterprises (1972) to market worms and worm bins. She added Flower Press (1976) to publish books and videos.

Mary had unique credentials for her work with worms. She taught high school biology for six years, three as academic faculty at Interlochen Arts Academy. Mary always preferred tramping in the woods with her students and collecting frogs from the pond to dissecting worms back in the lab.

Extensive post-graduate work in zoology prepared Mary for interacting with scientists at a level few worm growers achieve. She coordinated the highly successful *Workshop on the Role of Earthworms in Stabilization of Organic Residues,* compiling its proceedings. She also hosted the *Vermillenium* in 2000 which drew participants from 17 countries. Her participation in major worm conferences in the Philippines, England, France, Ireland, and the U.S., kept her current on state-of-the-art research. Mary toured Australia and New Zealand, where she was a popular speaker. There she visited with students in Kalangadoo, South Australia, as the "Worm Woman from Kalamazoo"—a highlight of her trip DownUnder.

Her diverse activities included publishing over 30 articles on solid waste-related issues. She co-authored *Worms Eat Our Garbage: Classroom Activities for a Better Environment* with Mary Frances Fenton and Barbara Loss Harris in 1993. Then in 1995, she produced the educational video, *Wormania!,* incorporating footage of worms on wet, rainy nights. Her **Worm-a-way®** is protected by U.S. and Canadian patents.

Mary died May 5, 2005. She was posthumously awarded the National Recycling Coalition's Recycler of the Year 2005, Lifetime Achievement.

Her legacy lives on at http://www.wormwoman.com.